RAILWAYS AR
WAKEFIELD AND
PONTEFRACT

John Farline
Peter Cookson

Published by Wyvern Publications, 50 Long Meadow, Skipton, North Yorkshire.
Text Copyright © J. E. Farline and P. Cookson.

Designed by Wyvern Publications.
Typeset and Printed by the Pindar Group of Companies, Scarborough, North Yorkshire.

Introduction

The railway system of what now comprises the Wakefield Metropolitan District was until relatively recently very complex, and included lines owned either fully or jointly by six different major Companies. In addition to these, there were many colliery systems which ranged in size from short tramways to the considerable operations of the East & West Yorkshire Union Railway. Local engineering companies, such as E Green & Son and Charles Roberts (now Procor (UK) Ltd) also had quite extensive systems. It is not possible within the confines of this volume to give a detailed and comprehensive history of the railways in the area. What we have tried to show is the complexity and variety of the railway system by the use of photographs and to give brief historical sketches of each of the lines, with emphasis on the major traffic centres. We would like to take this opportunity to thank all the photographers who have contributed material for use in this book (most of it previously unpublished). We should also express our gratitude to Mr Derek Griffith and Mr Jeff Hodgson for their assistance with information on the GNR main line and to Mrs Beryl Cookson for typing the manuscript.

John Farline   Alverthorpe
Peter Cookson   Pontefract
                                                1 August 1984

Contents

At Whitwood Junction near Methley, a short mineral branch ran into the pottery district of Whitwood Mere (Castleford) to serve various industrial premises including the Laporte Acids Plant. For many years class 'J71' and 'J72' 0-6-0T were based at Normanton for shunting this branch and the photograph shows 'J72' No 68726 at the terminus with a train of acid tanks returning to Whitwood Junction
P COOKSON

The first station to carry the name Wakefield was built by the North Midland Railway on its route from Derby to Leeds, being located at Oakenshaw just south of the Wakefield to Doncaster road. This was re-named Oakenshaw in 1841 when the Manchester & Leeds Railway built its own station at Kirkgate. The Manchester & Leeds Railway extended its line to Goose Hill Junction on the North Midland Railway (near Normanton) in October 1840 and in connection with this Henry Clarkson, the Wakefield surveyor, was contracted to act as a valuer and buyer of land including that which was required in his home town. The M & LR station at Wakefield was to be built at Kirkgate and to reach this site the railway had to be carried on a series of embankments and viaducts including arches over the street of Kirkgate itself. One of the most important cases of litigation during the building of the line concerned the bridging of Kirkgate. The Aire & Calder Navigation Company had made strong opposition to the construction of the M & LR and obtained an injunction from the Court of Chancery to stop the work on the viaduct. The A & CN contended that a viaduct, as detailed in the M & LR Act, should give an opening over the entire street and not, as the M & LR proposed, only over the roadway with smaller arches at each side for pedestrians. The case went in favour of the M & LR and the viaduct construction was completed.

The contract for building Kirkgate station was given to Child & Squires in June 1840. The station they built was a very basic affair and it received considerable criticism from waiting passengers. One of the principal porters at Kirkgate at this time was a well known local character named Dicky Dickens. He was renowned for ensuring that passengers were warned to keep clear of approaching trains but ironically forgot his own advice and was knocked down and killed by a passing train. An accident occurred on 8 November 1838 at the point where the newly constructed viaduct to the west of Kirkgate crossed over Ings Road. A horse drawn train of heavily loaded wagons was

crossing the viaduct when the sides of the arch over the road suddenly gave way. This arch and the ones at each side collapsed bringing down the train with them. The men in charge of the wagons and all of the horses were killed. The inspector of construction work had a narrow escape being struck by some of the brickwork as he ran away.

In 1849 the L & Y constructed a wagon lift to the west of Kirkgate to enable wagons to be moved between the viaduct carrying the main line and Thornes Wharf. The wharf had a railway yard which was connected to Smithson's tramway (see industrial section). In 1853 the L & Y agreed with the GNR to appoint a joint committee for the management of Kirkgate station and to rebuild it. The station building we see today was completed in 1857 and included a train shed with an all over roof. The station buildings remained generally in their original condition until 1972 when during March and April, the train shed roof was removed, the work taking five Sundays to complete. At the same time the buildings on the up platform were demolished. Fortunately, the main station building has been retained and in recent times, sand blasted to reveal the colour of the original stonework.

In April 1848 the Lancashire & Yorkshire Railway (successor to the M & L) commenced service on its line from Wakefield to Goole. This had been constructed by the contractor Joseph Thornton (a Wakefield man) on behalf of the Wakefield, Pontefract & Goole Railway. In 1847 the GNR had obtained running powers over the WP & G to Wakefield, and also, the WP & G had amalgamated with the L & Y. The Goole line was officially opened on 25 March 1848 with festive atmosphere at all of the towns along the line and at Wakefield and Pontefract the bells of the parish churches were rung throughout the day. A special train of twenty four carriages was run from Wakefield to Goole drawn by two engines decorated with flags, and at Pontefract an additional engine and twenty six carriages were attached! The WP & G also built a branch to Askern where it

The very first Wakefield station was on the North Midland Railway and was re-named Oakenshaw when the Manchester & Leeds Railway opened its own station at Kirkgate. It was situated just south of the present bridge over the Midland line on the Wakefield to Doncaster Road.

CITY OF WAKEFIELD M D ARCHIVES GOODCHILD LOAN MSS.

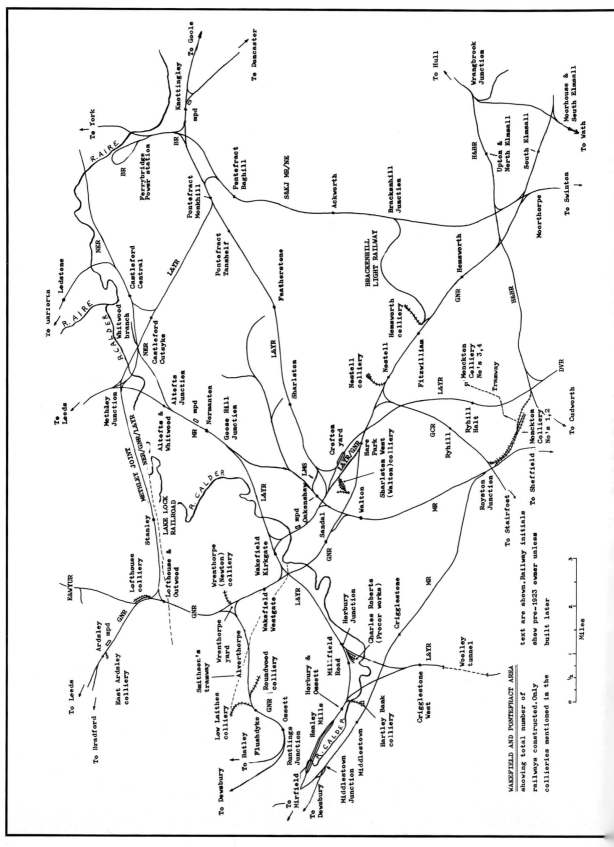

WAKEFIELD AND PONTEFRACT AREA
showing total number of
railways constructed.Only
collieries mentioned in the

text are shown.Railway initials
show pre-1923 owner unless
built later

Miles
0   ½   1   2   3

To Goole
To Doncaster
To York
To Hull
Wrangbrook Junction
Moorhouse & South Elmsall
To Wath
To Swinton
Upton & North Elmsall
South Elmsall
H&BR
Moorthorpe
Knottingley
mpd
BR
BR
Ferrybridge Power station
Pontefract Monkhill
Pontefract Baghill
S&KJ MR/NE
Ackworth
Brackenhill Junction
BRACKENHILL LIGHT RAILWAY
Hemsworth
GNR
H&BR
To Carlton
Ledstone
NER
R.AIRE
R.AIRE
Castleford Central
L&YR
Pontefract Tanshelf
Featherstone
L&YR
Sharlston
Nostell colliery
Nostell
Hemsworth colliery
Fitzwilliam
L&YR
Monckton Colliery No's 3,4
Tramway
DVR
To Cudworth
To Leeds
R.CALDER
Whitwood branch
NER
Castleford Cutsyke
Normanton
MR/O mpd
Goose Hill Junction
Crofton yard
Hare Park
Sharlston West (Walton)colliery
GCR
Ryhill
MR
Ryhill Halt
Monckton Colliery No's 1,2
To Sheffield
To Stairfoot
Methley Junction
Altofts & Whitwood
Altofts Junction
WETHLEY JOINT NER/GNR/L&YR
Stanley
LAKE LOCK RAILROAD
R.CALDER
L&YR
LMS
L&YR/GNR
Oakenshaw
Walton
Sandal
mpd
Royston Junction
E&WYUR
Lofthouse colliery
Lofthouse & Outwood
Wrenthorpe (Newton) colliery
Wakefield Kirkgate
GNR
Horbury Junction
Charles Roberts (Procor works)
Crigglestone
MR
To Ardsley
mpd
GNR
Wrenthorpe yard
Alverthorpe
Wakefield Westgate
L&YR
Millfield Road
Crigglestone West
L&YR
Woolley tunnel
To Leeds
To Bradford
Smithson's tramway
Low Laithes colliery
GNR
Roundwood colliery
Ossett
Horbury & Ossett
Healey Mills
Hartley Bank colliery
To Batley
Flushdyke
Runtlings Junction
Middlestown Junction
Middlestown
R.CALDER
To Dewsbury
To Mirfield
To Dewsbury
East Ardsley colliery
To Dewsbury

made an end-on connection with the GNR. It was from this point that the GNR was able to use its running powers to Wakefield. The WP & G is covered in section 5 of this book.

In October 1857 the GNR began working into Leeds over a viaduct which left the L & Y at Ings Road to join the Bradford, Wakefield & Leeds Railway at the new Westgate station which was a converted private house on the south side of Westgate. From 1866 the GNR used the West Riding & Grimsby Joint line from Doncaster to Westgate. However, Kirkgate remained a joint station up to nationalization and GNR/LNER trains continued to make use of it.

In 1882 a line was built from Kirkgate to Hare Park on the WR & G allowing through working between the GNR and L & Y Calder Valley line. This was also useful for diverting trains from Westgate whenever there was a blockage between Westgate and Hare Park Junction. Before Healey Mills was built, the major motive power depot in the Wakefield area was located at Belle Vue, Wakefield, adjacent to the Wakefield, Pontefract & Goole line to the east of Kirkgate. This depot, which closed on 3 June 1967, was the third Wakefield engine shed to be built during the period 1847 to 1967. The first was erected just to the east of Kirkgate in the vee formed by the lines to Normanton and Goole. It measured 125ft by 85ft and had five through roads, three of these giving access to a 36ft turntable. When the GNR began to use Kirkgate, they suggested to the L & Y that a new jointly owned shed should be built but the L & Y did not accept this idea and the GNR had to use the existing facilities. Around 1880 the first shed was demolished and replaced by a single ended ten road shed which was situated nearby. However, as Wakefield was the major motive power depot of the L & Y east of the Pennines, its allocation of locomotives continued to increase and by the mid 1880s totalled around 100. To cope with this large number, a new ten road shed was built at Belle Vue in 1893 and with modifications, this lasted until the end of steam. In 1930 improvements were made by the LMS which included renewal of the pits, new staff accommodation and the opening up of the end wall to make a through shed. The yard layout was re-arranged and ash disposal and coaling facilities were installed. The 200 tons capacity coaling plant was a prominent landmark until it was overshadowed by the cooling towers of the adjacent power station which were built in the early 1950s. A 70ft diameter vacuum operated turntable was installed close to the Wakefield–Doncaster road and this was served by eight tracks from the shed. During 1954 the shed roof was replaced by British Railways. The previous roof had, surprisingly, lasted from the time that the shed was built. Wakefield mpd was predominantly freight and throughout its life always had a large allocation of heavy goods locomotives including L & Y 0-6-0s, LMS Class '7F' 0-8-0s and finally, 'WD' 2-8-0s. The biggest available freight locomotives were used for trains along the Dearne Valley Railway and before nationalization double-heading was quite common. This line became the preserve of the 'WD' 2-8-0s after the second world war but towards the end of steam, a variety of different classes made occasional sorties down to Grimethorpe including 'Royal Scots'. Passenger workings were mainly of a local nature to Leeds, Barnsley, Sowerby Bridge etc. During L & Y and LMS days these were often worked by L & Y 2-4-2 radial tanks of which there were over a dozen allocated to the shed for many years. One passenger working requires special mention. This was the service along the Dearne Valley line from Kirkgate to Edlington (near Doncaster) which commenced on 3 June 1912 and was withdrawn on 10 September 1951. Up to the start of the second world war a Hughes steam rail motor was used, but this was replaced by an ex-LYR 2-4-2T attached to a rail motor coach which had been given an additional bogie. Motive power used in post nationalization days was an ex-LMS Ivatt 2-6-2T (No's 41283/4) fitted for push-pull work and it is interesting to note that the original Hughes coach was used to the end. Although very few passengers ever used these trains (the majority embarking at Ryhill halt) they managed to attain a certain notoriety as possibly one of the most ramshackle train services in the country. They also acquired nicknames. 'Titanic' was a well known name for the rail motors but the villagers of Ryhill also christened the push-pull trains 'Little Billy'. Passenger workings along the DVR were limited to excursions to Blackpool and Cleethorpes after the withdrawal of the push-pull service. Wakefield shed remained active nearly to the end of the steam with 75 engines still working in April 1966. However by the end of that year only 9 were left in steam, these being 7 Class 'B1' 4-6-0s and 2 Class '6P' 4-6-0 (No's 45694 **Bellerophon** and 45739 **Ulster**. At the present time the ex L & Y line is one of the

Crofton East Junction with WD 2-8-0 No 90420 running towards Crofton West Junction and Kirkgate with a load of timber from Goole docks to Whitham's sidings. The lines on the right lead to Crofton South Junction and Crofton yard.   R WALKER

busiest in the area with most of the traffic being freight, in particular, "merry go round" coal trains bound for the power stations to the east of Wakefield. Passenger trains are also seen but consist mainly of diesel multiple units heading to and from Barnsley and Huddersfield.

About 4 miles to the west of Wakefield is the village of Horbury and it was from Horbury Junction that the L & Y opened its line to Barnsley in 1850. Originally single track this was doubled in 1855 except for the section through the 1745 yards Woolley tunnel, the third longest on the L & Y. A second Woolley tunnel was opened in 1902 plus an additional line from Crigglestone to Horbury & Ossett. The railway wagon manufacturing company of Charles Roberts built its works alongside the Barnsley branch when it moved from its original site at Ings Road, Wakefield (see industrial section) and it is interesting to note that during the second world war six gangs of men were employed to camouflage the tracks against enemy attack. The camouflage was removed only when a train was due. The reason behind this work was that Charles Roberts was contracted to build armoured tanks for the War Department. Horbury Junction station opened in 1850 but was replaced by Horbury Millfield Road in 1927. Beyond Horbury Junction on the main line, was Horbury & Ossett station which had passenger access from the bridge carrying the Wakefield to Huddersfield road over the railway. Between 1892 and 1927 various sections of the line from Kirkgate to Healey Mills were widened including opening out the 128 yards Horbury tunnel and the conversion to an embankment of a 16 arch viaduct, to the west of Kirkgate. Where the line passed under the GNR '99 arches' viaduct, three tracks were placed through one arch and the fourth through an adjacent arch where it was necessary to lay the rails at a lower level. Through Horbury & Ossett station there were six tracks due to goods loops being added to the outside of the formation in both directions. In 1963 a hump marshalling yard was opened at Healey Mills replacing 13 smaller yards. The new yard extended approximately from Thornhill Midland Junction to just west of the site of Horbury & Ossett station. The River Calder was in the way and a diversion was made so that an area of 140 acres could be used. Healey Mills was designed to handle 4,500 wagons per day and included a diesel depot and power signal box. The four main line tracks between Thornhill Midland Junction and Horbury & Ossett were re-aligned so that the eastbound ones ran around the north of the yard and the westbound around the south. One of the yards replaced by Healey Mills was Crofton which was sited to the south of Wakefield on the line built by the L & Y to connect with the Dearne Valley Railway. Crofton yard had been built to act as a distribution centre for coal brought in from the West and South Yorkshire coalfields. Trains of 50 to 80 wagons travelled from Crofton along the DVR to Grimethorpe where they were split into smaller units for the use of individual collieries. The return trips were made with trains made up to the equivalent of 33 – standard 16 ton loaded wagons. At Crofton trains were marshalled for various destinations including Goole (for export coal), Stourton (for sending on to Scotland) and Crewe, plus many more.

One interesting working was the local one from Nostell colliery. This train would travel up the GNR main line and bear off at Hare Park Junction as far as the junction with the WP & G at Crofton. It would go beyond the junction then reverse up to Crofton West Junction and on to the Deane Valley line. There was a gradient up to Crofton South Junction and, for this reason, loaded trains from Nostell were restricted to 25 to 30 wagons. Before the engine set back to propel its train from Crofton West, it was necessary to ensure that there was a clear road at Crofton South so that it did not have to stop. This was because there was great difficulty in re-starting a train on the gradient once it had come to a standstill. The train would run straight through Crofton yard and once clear, reverse again and enter the yard as though it was running in off the Dearne Valley line. Before the closure of Crofton yard a considerable amount of traffic was transferred to Brierley Sidings on the connecting line between the DVR and the Hull & Barnsley Railway near Shafton. The working of outward bound traffic from the yard ended at the beginning of 1966 but it was used for the stabling of empty wagons up to closure on 11 July 1966.

Former L&YR 4-4-2, LMS No 10327 stands at Wakefield Kirkgate on 6 October 1926.   A P HERBERT, courtesy R HERBERT

LMS Class 2MT 2-6-0 No 6408 enters Kirkgate from the east with a pick-up goods which probably originated from Goole. Although the photograph was taken on 29 April 1949 the locomotive and tender are still in LMS post-war livery.　H C CASSERLEY

Occasionally, trains are diverted from Westgate via Kirkgate and then back onto the GN line at Hare Park Junction. This 1938 scene shows Class 'A4' 4-6-2 No 4495 *Golden Fleece* passing Wakefield East box. Part of Kirkgate station can be seen in the left background.
　G HALLOS COLLECTION

LNER 'C14' 4-4-2T No 7444 waits to depart from Kirkgate on 11 March 1948 with a train for Westgate. The engine has brought the train in from Westgate and then run round to form the Kirkgate–Bradford Exchange service via the Ossett branch.
　H C CASSERLEY

Stanier Class 4 2-6-4T No 42650 departs from the west end of Kirkgate with a local stopping train for Bradford. 'Crab' 2-6-0 No 42846 of Saltley shed waits for the arrival of a westbound express to which it would be added as pilot, presumably to work back to its home depot.

S PITCHFORTH COLLECTION

Super power for the 8.25am Leeds to Doncaster stopping train on 2 August 1961 seen entering Kirkgate at 9.00am from Westgate. The engine is Class 'A2' 4-6-2- No 60533 *Happy Knight*. The train formation is interesting, consisting of a Gresley articulated suburban set at the front and a similar steel panelled set at the rear. The train would continue from Kirkgate along the line to Hare Park Junction where it would re-join the Westgate to Doncaster line.

P COOKSON

A grimy Class 9F 2-10-0 with a rebuilt Crosti boiler heads from Kirkgate to Healey Mills. The building in the right background is the housing for a lift which transported wagons from the railway down to a yard at Thornes Wharf next to the River Calder. C MARSH

A 'Black 5' 4-6-0 takes the route from Kirkgate to Westgate at Ings Road Junction. This was the original GNR entry into Westgate before the Doncaster–Westgate direct line was laid. Note the colour light signal on the left with a cross on it signifying ''not in use''. The strange thing about this installation was that the signal was never used. The track from this junction to where it connects with the Doncaster–Westgate line has now been singled. C MARSH

'A1' 4-6-2 No 2555 *Centenary* tdakes the line from Kirkgate to Hare Park Junction with the up "Queen of Scots Pullman". Part of the LMS motive power depot is in the background. The photograph was taken in 1938. G HALLOS COLLECTION

A scene which was typical of Wakefield shed during BR steam days. WD 2-8-0s line up with No 90047 in the foreground. In the left background can be seen the lodging house. A ROBINSON

Wakefield shed in LMS days with ex-L&Y locos very much in evidence. The building in the background is the loco crew lodging house. This view changed drastically when the Wakefield power station was built during the early 1950s.
G HALLOS COLLECTION

A typical line-up of Class WD 2-8-0 locomotives at Wakefield not long before closure of the shed.   D COOK

'Black 5' in trouble at Crofton yard. No 44853 is prepared for lifting by the local breakdown crew. The breakdown train is in the background behind the 'WD' 2-8-0. The errant Class '5' had run through the buffers at the Permanent Way Depot on 28 March 1965.

R EARNSHAW

Former L&YR rail-motor No 10616 stands in the centre road at Wakefield Kirkgate between trips on the Dearne Valley service to Edlington.

LYR SOCIETY

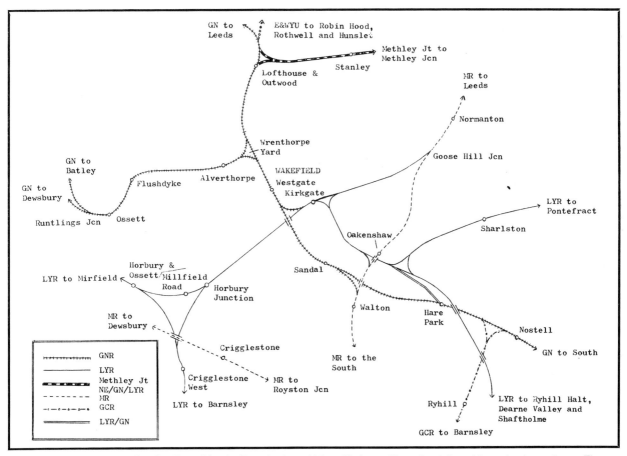

An L&Y 0-4-4T approaches Woolley Tunnel (on the Barnsley branch) from Horbury with a rake of six and four-wheeler carriages. The tunnel had two separate bores and in the left foreground can be seen the line which has emerged from the other bore built at a later date.

LYR SOCIETY

Millfield Road station was built by the LMS in 1927 when Horbury Junction station was closed. Situated on the ex-L&Y main line between Horbury & Ossett station and Horbury Junction Millfield Road was built as an island platform with access from the adjacent road overbridge. The photograph was taken looking towards Horbury & Ossett before closure on 6 November 1961.   G HALLOS COLLECTION

On the main line from Lancashire ex-WD 2-8-0 No 90339 heads east from Healey Mills and is about to pass under the Wakefield–Huddersfield road with a train of empty mineral wagons. The buildings in the right background belonged to Wagon Repairs Ltd which became part of the Procor group.   R HEPWORTH

Class '8F' 2-8-0 No 48710 runs through Horbury & Ossett station on its way to Healey Mills yard. This locomotive was one of the batch built by the Southern Railway's Brighton works in 1944 for use by the LNER. They were classified by the LNER as '06'. Behind the front end of the engine can be seen the high level entrance to the station from the Wakefield–Huddersfield road.　　R HEPWORTH

Class 9F 2-10-0 No 92006 heads west through Horbury Cutting on 29 April 1966. This was the location of Horbury tunnel before the former L&Y main line was widened to four tracks in the 1920s.　　M BRADLEY

2 | Around Wakefield Westgate

Regarded by many as being the most interesting of the Wakefield stations, Westgate was opened on its present site in May 1867. Planned by the West Riding & Grimsby Joint Railway in 1864 it was agreed that the West Yorkshire Railway (originally Bradford, Wakefield & Leeds) would be able to use it and therefore dispense with its own existing station which was located in a former private house on the south side of Westgate. The Midland Railway was also allowed access. However during 1865, after construction had begun, the GNR acquired the WYR and came to an agreement with the Manchester, Sheffield & Lincolnshire Railway to take over the WR & G. The GNR also had an agreement which allowed the MS & L and the Midland to rent the adjacent goods station and yard which were opened in 1868. Ultimately, all three Companies agreed to share the cost of both the passenger and goods stations which were put under the control of a joint committee created by an Act of 1867 which also confirmed that the L & Y could continue to use Westgate as it had done since making an agreement with the BW & L in 1854. The station was built on top of a series of arches and it was possible to walk from Westgate through to Back Lane underneath these arches. A water main and various signalling and communication cables were eventually installed under the platforms through the arches and this area was very useful from a maintenance point of view. Access to the underside of the station was gained from an arched doorway built into the abutment wall of the bridge over Westgate. It was also possible to use this as an entrance to the booking office until 1939 when the area beneath the station was made into an air raid shelter. The most outstanding feature of the station was the Italianate clock tower which reached a height of 97 feet above the adjacent street. The clock was operated by weights which were hung inside two cast iron tubes mounted on the city side of the tower. Inside the tower was an iron spiral staircase which gave access to the clock chamber. The clock had a mechanism which enabled it to strike the hour of the day and was kept running by being wound up on Sunday mornings. It was also fitted with gas lighting but this was removed in 1939 when war started, presumably as a fire precaution. In the outside wall of the station adjacent to No 4 bay platform, was a doorway which gave access to a wooden staircase; this led down to Love Lane and was used by the Wakefield Prison authorities whenever they had to bring a prisoner on to the station for transportation by rail. The staircase went out of use and was removed during the 1950s. The girder bridge carrying the tracks over Westgate was renewed in 1950 and this resulted in a different appearance – the new girders were higher and had square ends compared with the low profile and rounded ends of their predecessors. The station frontage, like the clock tower, had an Italianate façade which, along with the rest of the buildings on the up side was demolished in 1967 to be replaced by the present-day structure. Previous to these alterations, the original awnings over the platforms and the entrance had been replaced by modern cantilevered structures. At the same time the footbridge was lifted so that it would clear the new awnings and also be suitable for any future electrification scheme. Considering the amount of demolition which took place on the up side it is surprising to find that the down side buildings are virtually unaltered, although the various rooms have been put to different uses throughout the years. During steam days, Westgate was well known for the complex movement of passenger stock in and around the station area caused by the need to add and remove the Bradford portions of trains to and from Kings Cross.

On the down side of the station were two bay platforms used by trains for Dewsbury and Batley via Wrenthorpe South junction, Alverthorpe, Flushdyke and Ossett. The original line built by the BW & L between 1862 and 1864, curved round to Batley at Runtlings Lane but, in 1880, the GNR (successor to the BW & L) completed the Dewsbury loop so that trains then ran to Batley via Dewsbury. The line had some severe gradients, particularly beyond Ossett, and locomotives were required to work hard in both directions. Between Alverthorpe and Flushdyke stations, at the top of the climb over Low Laithes, were connections to collieries at Roundwood and Low Laithes, both having long since disappeared. On the Wakefield side of Flushdyke station there were sidings for the marshalling of wagons from both collieries. The biggest station between Westgate and Dewsbury was Ossett. It was situated on the south west side of the Station Road overbridge with a goods yard on the north east side. An unusual feature was that access to the platform area could be made by either walking up or down a staircase from the streets which the line went under and over at each end of the station. There were two signal boxes, Ossett East and West. The West box was destroyed by fire in the early hours of 10 March 1956 and was never replaced. The goods yard and warehouse dealt with a considerable amount of traffic, much of it being for the manufacturing companies based in the town. Ossett station, along with the rest of the line closed in September 1964.

On the up side at the north end of Westgate station was the GC/Midland goods yard. This included a large warehouse which was entered by five sets of tracks. At the other end only four tracks emerged, each being fitted with a wagon turntable. Beyond the goods shed, adjacent to Cliff Lane, were located a number of cattle pens. Next to the boundary wall, alongside Cliff Hill, was the three road straight engine shed with a turntable and coaling facility used by the GCR/MR. It was still possible, up to recent times, to see the outline of the turntable. The goods warehouse was demolished in 1970 and today a much simplified yard is used as a terminal for car transporter trains.

Between Wrenthorpe South, West and North junctions was located Wrenthorpe yard. This was used to marshal local freight workings, particularly coal trains from the GCR Barnsley branch and the East & West Yorkshire Union Railway. There were also fish trains from Grimsby and loads of steel from Frodingham. One interesting working was to the North Eastern Railway yard at Gascoigne Wood. This was a coal train off the GCR Barnsley branch which was re-marshalled at Wrenthorpe and then sent to Lofthouse South junction to reach its destination via the Methley Joint line. In its latter days it was usually hauled by a Class 'J27' 0-6-0 and was the only goods train allowed to leave the yard immediately before any passenger workings out of Westgate. The train was nicknamed "Geordie" by the men at Wrenthorpe yard. Midway between the junctions on the up side was a spur to Wrenthorpe colliery which passed under Bradford Road to the site where the present-day offices of the Wakefield Metropolitan Council are situated. Continuing north in the direction of Leeds, the line curves towards Ardsley near the site of the recently closed Lofthouse Colliery. It was at this point, adjacent to the original GNR Lofthouse & Wrenthorpe Station, that the Methley Joint Railway branched off.

The final place on the northbound run from Wakefield which falls into the area covered by this book is Ardsley. It is difficult to believe that this village, which now has only the two

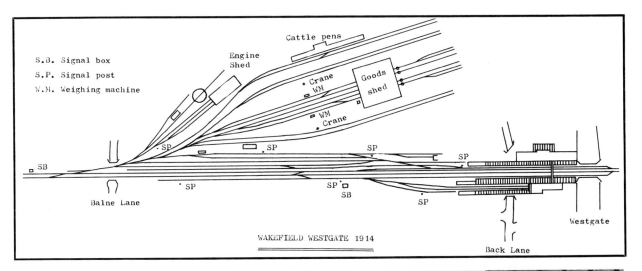

WAKEFIELD WESTGATE 1914

A turn of the century scene at Westgate. Great Northern Railway 4-4-2T No 1017 (LNER Class 'C12') stands at the down platform with what is probably a Wakefield Kirkgate to Bradford (Via the Ossett branch) stopping train. The locomotive is in immaculate condition and attached to what appears to be a set of GNR six-wheeled carriages. No 1017 was one of a batch of ten built specially for use in the West Riding.
D B WOODWARD
        COLLECTION

Former GNR Class 'J6' 0-6-0 No 64271 sorts out a Bradford portion at Westgate ready for moving to the yard prior to attaching it to a Leeds to Kings Cross train when it arrives. The two centre coaches are an ex-tourist stock twin set which originally carried green and cream livery.
P COOKSON
        COLLECTION

The crew of an unidentified class 'J6' 0-6-0 have a chat as their engine hauls a southbound mixed goods towards Westgate. Note how cars (Ford Anglia's) were transported in the days before specialist vehicles were introduced. S PITCHFORTH COLLECTION

Class 'J39' 0-6-0 No 64839 heads north through Westgate with a mixed goods whilst Stanier class 4 2-6-4T No 42650 stands in the background with its safety valves blowing off. S PITCHFORTH COLLECTION

tracks of the Wakefield to Leeds line passing through it, was once an important railway centre which had an 8-road engine shed, a 4-platform station, an extensive marshalling yard and a branch off the main line to Bradford. Ardsley shed was mainly responsible for freight traffic. Considerable goods workings were made from East Ardsley Colliery and East Ardsley Ironworks, the latter facility being particularly important to the North Eastern Railway which obtained running powers to work over the GNR from the Methley Joint line to the works. Marshalling of trains took place in the yard which served a similar purpose to that at Wrenthorpe. The shed was famous for its allocation of Class 'J50' 0-6-0T engines which had the name 'Ardsley Tanks' bestowed upon them. A few express passenger engines were allocated to Ardsley including the last of the GCR 'Immingham' class 4-6-0s – LNER No 1482, which survived until 1950 still decked out in LNER apple green livery. A public footpath ran between the main running lines and the sidings from the Falls bridge, adjacent to the shed, to the station, and although fenced off for obvious reasons was an excellent vantage point for local enthusiasts. The Ardsley complex lasted until near the end of steam with the station being closed in 1964 and the shed in 1966.

The 'Wakefield Journal & Examiner' of 31 July 1863 reported that ''on 24th July 1863 the turning of the first sod of the Methley Branch Railway was carried out by the chairman of the West Yorkshire Railway Company (previously Bradford, Wakefield & Leeds Railway) in a field near to Lofthouse and Wrenthorpe station. Many shareholders were brought to the event in special trains. The Branch to be 5½ miles long will run through Lofthouse, Stanley, Lake Lock where there will be a station, Bottomboat, Foxholes and Methley. It will connect with the L & Y and NER just beyond Methley. The contract has been given to Messrs Bray and Sons who have undertaken to complete the work in twelve months at a cost of £75,000. The works were blessed by Rev R Burrell, the vicar of Stanley, and the first sod was then dug by Mr Firth, the chairman of the West Yorkshire Railway Co." The line was completed in 1865 but passenger services did not begin until 1 May 1869. The GNR

(after absorbing the WYR) had joint ownership with the L & Y and NER, and Lofthouse South junction became the closest point to Wakefield under NER jurisdiction. Stations were built at Lofthouse & Outwood (joining up with the existing station), Stanley, and Methley, but there does not appear to have been one at Lake Lock in spite of the aims mentioned in the above report. Trains were now able to work through from Leeds and Wakefield to Castleford over the Methley Joint. It also proved useful for freight working to and from Ardsley yard. In later years the line was a link for holiday trains to and from the east coast resorts. Banking was often necessary up to Methley when heading east and to Lofthouse in the opposite direction. The village of Stanley, two miles north of Wakefield, is in one of the finest rhubarb growing areas in Britain and before the second world war considerable traffic was handled at the station due to special trains being run to take this produce to the markets. During the second world war a loading platform was built so that coal lorries working from a nearby open cast mine could tip their loads directly into railway wagons. The line was closed to passengers from Lofthouse North junction to Methley Joint Junction on 2 November 1964 along with Stanley station. Lofthouse & Outwood and Methley Junction stations had already been closed in 1960 and passenger services from Lofthouse South had been terminated in 1957. However, a goods service was retained between the Lofthouse junction and the Newmarket Colliery branch until 5 April 1965.

From the sidings of Lofthouse Colliery emerged the East & West Yorkshire Union Railway. This had been born as an attempt to make a connection between the GNR at Lofthouse and the Hull & Barnsley Railway at Drax, but it eventually evolved into a network of lines connecting the collieries of the Charlesworth family in the area around Robin Hood and Rothwell. Connections were made with the GNR at Lofthouse and the Midland at Stourton, Leeds. Goods working commenced in 1891 and a short-lived passenger service was run between Robin Hood and Leeds Wellington during 1904 but it was a complete disaster and only lasted nine months. The entire E & WYUR system had been closed by 1966.

Class 'B1' 4-6-0 No 61016 *Inyala* approaches Westgate from the north with an inspection saloon. A set of articulated suburban carriages can be seen in the background and behind these was the site of the Great Central Railway engine shed. The turntable pit could be seen up to recent times.
C MARSH

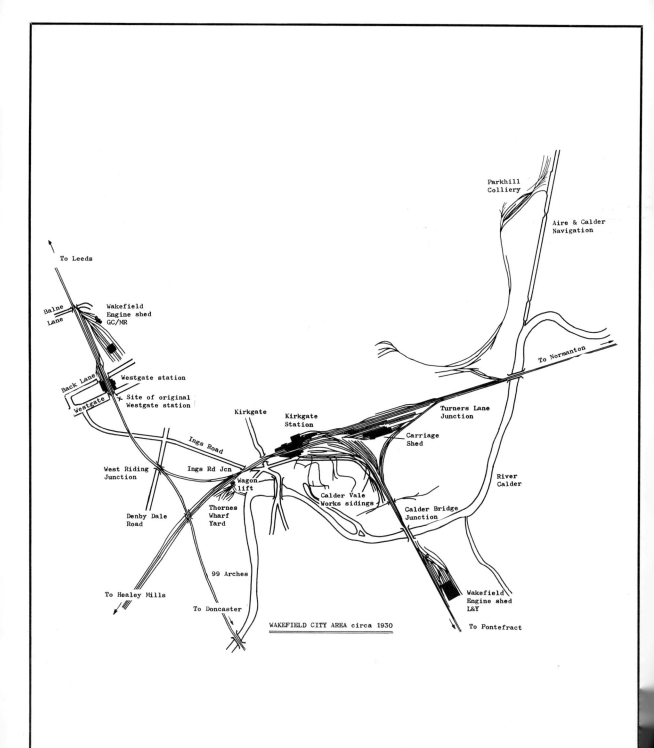

WAKEFIELD CITY AREA circa 1930

In this circa 1958 photograph the Bradford portion of an express from Kings Cross has been detached from the Leeds coaches and the train is seen leaving Westgate for Bradford behind Class 'B1' 4-6-0 No 61011 *Waterbuck* (then allocated to Ardsley).   C MARSH

A busy scene at the north end of Westgate in the early 1950s. Class 'B17' 4-6-0 No 61640 *Somerleyton Hall* sets off for Leeds with an express from Kings Cross. This was an unusual locomotive type at Westgate and was possibly put on at Doncaster as a replacement for a failed 'Pacific'. The J39' 0-6-0 on the right is waiting to take out the Bradford portion detached from the 'B17's train.   C MARSH

The down 'West Riding' leaves Westgate behind Class 'A1' 4-6-2 No 60131 *Osprey* of Copley Hill shed. The first six coaches are from the original 'West Riding Limited' streamlined train of the 1930s. The photograph was probably taken during 1950 or early 1951 because on 14 July 1951 some of the streamlined stock was destroyed when the down 'West Riding' caught fire at Huntingdon. Two articulated twins, Nos 45811 and 45812 were burnt out plus an ex-'Coronation' set, Nos 1737 and 1738. Although some publications have stated that part of the 'West Riding Limited' stock was destroyed during wartime, this was not so and the whole train survived intact until the Huntingdon incident. After that date, the 'West Riding' was equipped with all BR standard stock. C MARSH

Wrenthorpe South Junction 1950. Part of Wrenthorpe yard can be seen in the background. The line which curves to the left past the huts is part of the Westgate–Ossett–Batley branch. The locomotive is LNER Class 'B4' 4-6-0 No 1482 *Immingham*, which is being turned on the triangle formed by the main line and the junctions onto the branch. D GRIFFITH

Alverthorpe station on the GNR Westgate to Dewsbury and Batley branch. The track on the right divided beyond the gate to form two sidings. Notice the signals, particularly the one in front of the wooden station building which has its lamp and spectacle glasses mounted considerably lower down the post than the semaphore arm. The arm was for daylight sighting and the lamp for night-time sighting. It is thought that this photograph, looking towards Wakefield, was taken around 1910.

CITY OF WAKEFIELD M D ARCHIVES GOODCHILD LOAN MSS

Monday morning at Ossett on 31 August 1959 as Class 'J50' 0-6-0T No 68898 shunts the pick-up goods. The locomotive, an 'Ardsley Tank' has extended coal rails on the bunker. These were added to increase the coal capacity of the first ten locomotives but the remainder of the Class had larger size bunkers.

R HEPWORTH

A special train for the Ossett Trades & Labour Club annual outing arrives at Ossett with the empty stock double-headed by Class 'B1' 4-6-0s No 61189 *Sir William Gray* and 61318.
R HEPWORTH

Fairburn Class 4MT 2-6-4T No 42108 pulls away from Ossett with a Cleethorpes–Bradford train on 13 July 1963. The four carriages would have been detached from a Cleethorpes–Leeds train at Wakefield Westgate. It would be difficult to recognise this scene now as the railway has completely disappeared and the whole area has been built upon. The modern road of Towngate now runs in the cutting which the bridge crossed.
R HEPWORTH

Class 'J6' 0-6-0 No 64170 and an unidentified 'B1' 4-6-0 bring a Sunday excursion up the climb from Dewsbury at Runtlings Junction. The line on the right was the original route to Batley before the loop via Dewsbury was installed. The leading carriage is interesting as it is an ex-GER brake 3rd corridor. A ROBINSON

Class 'N1' 0-6-2T No 69471 arrives at Stanley with a local stopping train from Castleford to Leeds on 24 April 1954 Stanley station was on the Methley Joint Line and the train is crossing the Wakefield–Oulton road.
H C CASSERLEY

Class 'A2/2' 4-6-2 No 60506 *Wolf of Badenoch* heads to Leeds Central with a stopping train from Doncaster. In the background is the now closed Lofthouse Colliery. At this location a triangular junction was made with the Methley Joint Line and a branch of the East & West Yorkshire Union Railway also commenced from the colliery sidings. The locomotive was one of Thompson's rebuilds of Gresley's magnificent class 'P2' 2-8-2s. The leading vehicle is an ex-GNR milk van, the rest of the train being made up of Gresley standard suburban stock.
C MARSH

The best known of all the 'A4' locomotives – No 60022 *Mallard* was photographed in charge of a Leeds–Kings Cross train between Ardsley and Lofthouse in the early 1950s.
C MARSH

Ardsley Station looking towards Leeds and showing a 'K3' Class 2-6-0 No 61984 which had just worked off the Bradford line with an empty wagon train. Although four platforms still existed at this time only the two on the far right (i.e. Leeds lines) were in use. The two tracks in the foreground were the goods lines for the Bradford branch.   P COOKSON

LNER Class 'F4' 2-4-2T No 7104 arrives at Ardsley with a push-pull train from the Tingley branch. Although the date of the photograph is not known, the locomotive and coaches remained in this condition into early nationalization days. This push-pull set was also used on the Westgate–Castleford Central workings.
C H S OWEN/GCRS
          COLLECTION

The last surviving ex-Great Central Railway 4-6-0 (LNER Class 'B4') No 1482 *Immingham* was photographed shortly before withdrawal at Ardsley shed on 26 June 1950.   H C CASSERLEY

No 68869, a Class 'J52' 0-6-0T stops the traffic as it crosses the A61 Leeds to Wakefield road on the Thorpe branch of the East & West Yorkshire Union Railway. The photograph was taken looking towards Wakefield on 20 February 1961. P COOKSON

Robin Hood station building and signal cabin on the E&WYUR on 15 March 1961. P COOKSON

Class 'J6' No 64226 returns with a light load of one tank wagon from Stourton and pauses at Robin Hood station near to the site of the old engine shed; the water tower and water crane were all that was left when this 1961 photograph was taken.   P COOKSON

Austerity 0-6-0ST (LNER Class 'J94') No 68011 comes up the climb from the Newmarket branch on the E&WYUR on 15 March 1961.
P COOKSON

South of Westgate, the line built by the WR & G is supported by the so-called "99 arches" viaduct. It is not known how the viaduct came to have this name but local railwayman and enthusiast, Mr Jeff Hodgson, has made a study of the viaduct in an attempt to find out the exact number of arches and it is worth recording the results of his observations. Working from the south at Sandal, there are three brick arches, No's 1–3. These are followed by the bridge over the River Calder where a foundation stone is built into the abutments. This gives the information that the bridge was built by the Great Northern Railway, the engineers being J Fowler and J Fraser. The architects were J A & B Fraser and the resident engineer R S Clayton. The original cast iron bridge was replaced by a stronger structure in the 1930s. North of the river brick arches continue with No 4–57 and 59–67. Arch 58 is built of stone and carries the railway over Thornes Lane. The point where the GNR line crosses the L & Y should be the location of arch 68 but in fact, the line is supported by bridge number 64. It is presumed that arch 68, which must have been wider than the preceding ones, was replaced by the bridge when the L & Y main line was widened early this century. Three tracks go under the bridge, the fourth passing through arch 69. Arches 69–93, all built from brick, complete the viaduct built by the GNR. If the original arch number 68 is included then the total number of arches built was 93. If the line from Ings Road Junction to Westgate is considered there are additional arches as follows: 1–12 from the bridge over Denby Dale road. Arch 13 which was built at a skew angle over an old road called Lady Lane and arches 14–20 up to the Ings Road bridge. It is thought that the bridge over Denby Dale road was originally designated as an arch and with this included, the total number of arches built was 21. This gives two possible total numbers of arches; 93 if only the GNR viaduct from the south is considered and 114 if the earlier viaduct to the original Westgate station of the BW & L is included. After looking at all the preceding information, the question still remains unanswered as to why the GNR viaduct has always been known as "99 arches".

The first station out of Westgate was Sandal which was built adjacent to Agbrigg Road. Beyond the site of this station the line climbs up Sandal bank, eventually to pass under the Midland main line at Walton. Between Sandal station and Walton was a connecting line bearing off to the south which climbed up to join the Midland. As mentioned previously the first station to bear the name of Wakefield was located on the North Midland Railway line from Derby to Leeds, being located at Oakenshaw. This was renamed Oakenshaw in 1841 when the Manchester & Leeds Company built its station in Kirkgate. Oakenshaw remained in use up to 1870 when it closed to passengers being replaced by a new station further south which was named Sandal & Walton. This survived until 1960, having been re-named Walton in September 1951.

Surveys of the North Midland line had been undertaken by surveyors who lived in the vicinity of the proposed railway. One of these was Henry Clarkson (of Wakefield) who, in 1835, was given the contract for the section from Cudworth to Oakenshaw. The work was straightforward until Clarkson and his assistants entered the Chevet estate of Sir William Pilkington, near Walton. Pilkington refused to allow the survey to be done and Clarkson was told that he would be jailed if he set foot on the estate again. As a result of this warning the major part of the survey across the estate had to be done by triangulation from points on the public roads and footpaths which crossed it. There were further problems when levels had to be taken as this necessitated going on to the estate. As the landowner had posted look-outs during the daylight hours, Clarkson had to finish the job at night, but in fact did not enter the estate himself instead sending his assistants who managed to read the levelling staff by having a lantern shine on it. Such were the problems facing the early railway surveyors. Eventually, Sir William Pilkington gave in to the North Midland Railway when they offered an inflated price for his land and the line was officially opened on 30 June 1840 at the same time as the York and North Midland Railway from York to Altofts Junction.

To the north of Oakenshaw is Goose Hill Junction where the M & LR joined the NMR in October, 1840. The next station on the line is Normanton which, during the early years of the railway age, was one of the most important railway centres in England. It was a joint station, the cost being shared by the Y & NMR, the NMR and the M & LR, but managed by the NMR on its own. Normanton was well known for its hotel and refreshment rooms which served meals to passengers travelling on long distance expresses. The hotel was constructed from stone removed from one of the cuttings on the NMR and was connected directly to the station by a footbridge. The station originally consisted of two island platforms but was rebuilt in 1871 as a single island almost a quarter of a mile in length, being one of the longest in the country. There were also two double tracked bays built into each end of the platform. As traffic increased, two yards were developed on the west side of the station, these being separated by the bridge which carries Altofts Road. Across the main line tracks from the north yard was Normanton motive power depot. The first shed was opened in the early 1850s and built as a joint venture by the Midland and North Eastern Railways. The number of engines stabled there soon outgrew the available accommodation and in 1867 the Midland Railway opened a roundhouse which had 24 roads. The majority of the locomotives based there were Midland Railways with only 20% North Eastern. In 1884 the Midland built a five road straight shed for use by the L & Y. This was of a Midland design but the coal stage (built at the same time) was typical L & Y. A turntable was also installed. In November 1927 both sheds came under the control of the Midland Division of the LMS. In the late 1930s, the LMS added new coal and ash facilities and the roundhouse was removed. From the end of 1938 the LNER ceased to enjoy the facilities of the "joint" shed and from that time any LNER engines using the depot were charged an agreed rent. Normanton was primarily a freight shed and throughout its life the principal freight locomotives of the constituent companies and of the LMS were the major occupants. These included '3F' 0-6-0s of the L & Y, '4F' 0-6-0s of the Midland and '7F' 0-8-0s and '8F' 2-8-0s of the LMS. In post-nationalization days, as at Wakefield, the 'WD' 2-8-0s were seen in large numbers. From January 1957 Normanton came under the jurisdiction of the North Eastern Region of British Railways and the shed code was changed from 20D to 55E. The depot closed on 2 October 1967.

Various connections were made between the Midland line and other railways. There were connecting curves with the L & Y and the West Riding & Grimsby Joint Railway at Oakenshaw South and West Riding Junctions respectively. At Oakenshaw North Junction, in 1928, the LMS built a connection to the ex-Wakefield, Pontefract & Goole Railway at Crofton. In 1885, a

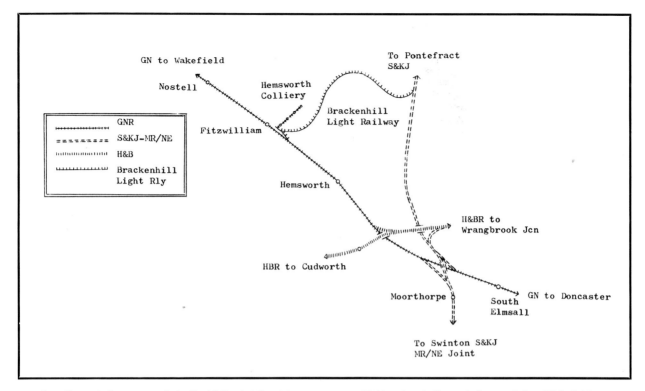

GNR
S&KJ-MR/NE
H&B
Brackenhill Light Rly

GN to Wakefield
Nostell
Hemsworth Colliery
Fitzwilliam
Brackenhill Light Railway
To Pontefract S&KJ
Hemsworth
H&BR to Wrangbrook Jcn
HBR to Cudworth
Moorthorpe
South Elmsall
GN to Doncaster
To Swinton S&KJ MR/NE Joint

spur from the main line was made by the Midland at Snydale junction to the north of Oakenshaw to serve the Don Pedro colliery near Loscoe with a branch off to Featherstone Main Colliery. Widening of the Midland line south of Snydale junction began in 1898 and eventually included the opening out of Chevet tunnel (near Walton) in 1923–5 to make what is reputed to be the deepest railway cutting in Britain, the maximum depth being about 100 feet. To the south of Chevet, the Midland built a branch line from Royston Junction to Thornhill Junction on the L & Y. This was meant to be the springboard for a direct route from St. Pancras to Bradford and eventually to Scotland but this idea did not materialise, and the branch was run by the Midland goods only. In 1909, the L & Y, which had an arrangement with the Midland, began a passenger service between Halifax and Sheffield utilizing the Thornhill branch with some of the trains including through carriages from Halifax and Bradford to St. Pancras. The Halifax to Sheffield service was maintained until 1946. There was a short period with a restored passenger service during 1960, but after that, regular passenger trains were withdrawn although a summer service survived until the autumn of 1967. The line was finally closed in 1968. A couple of lasting monuments to this Midland folly are the superb viaducts at Calder Grove and Horbury Bridge, but unfortunately, their future is uncertain.

Today, the Midland main line is no longer a major carrier of traffic and, the latest information to hand suggests that the line is to be severed south of Cudworth, reduced to two tracks from Cudworth to Oakenshaw, and the Oakenshaw to Goose Hill section removed altogether. The section from Goose Hill to Altofts Junction would only need to be double track instead of quadruple, and it has been suggested that a new "bus stop" station on a slightly different site should be provided at Normanton to replace the old one; however the West Yorkshire P T E has not yet given its support and the remains of the old station may yet survive a little longer. If these proposals are implemented there will be no more through working over the NMR and only the local dmu service from Leeds to Barnsley via Wakefield will use it.

But to return to the main line south from Wakefield Westgate. Just over 2 miles south of the junction with the Midland Railway near Walton is Hare Park Junction where the connecting line from the L & Y at Kirkgate joins the GNR. A short distance beyond Hare Park Junction was Hare Park & Crofton station which opened around 1885. Nostell was the next station on the GNR and it was just north of here, in 1882, that a triangular junction was made with the MS & L line from Barnsley. This had evolved from the Barnsley Coal Railway which had been taken over by the MS & L. The only station on this line which comes into the scope of this book was Ryhill (re-named Wintersett & Ryhill in 1927). The station handled both passenger and goods traffic although apart from special excursions the passenger service was withdrawn and the station closed in September 1930. The goods service on the line survived until the early 1960s.

Returning to the GNR, Nostell station had sidings serving the adjacent colliery and some of these survive today. Additional sidings and coal loading facilities have been built in recent years to serve a nearby opencast mine. Nostell station closed in 1951. The LNER built Fitzwilliam station, midway between Nostell and Hemsworth, in 1937 and this closed in 1967 but, in 1982 a new structure was built in a position slightly closer to Doncaster. This was one of the bus shelter and timber platform type of halts which have been subsidised by the West Yorkshire Passenger Transport Executive.

The passing of the Light Railways Act in 1896 made it possible for railways to be built to lighter constructional standards than had hitherto been allowed, and around the turn of the century this was made use of by many branch-line schemes which were able to take advantage of cheaper construction. One such was the Brackenhill Light Railway Company whose line ran from Brackenhill Junction on the S & K, to Hemsworth Colliery alongside the WR & G, near to Fitzwilliam Station. The Company was granted a Light Railway Order in March 1901, but the line was not completed until 1914 after many delays during which time another scheme was mooted which would have affected the history of railways in the

Pontefract area. The L & Y Company was keen to get a foothold into North Lincolnshire so as to take advantage of the traffic accruing from the ironstone mines of the district, much against the wishes and interests of the GCR which jealously regarded the area as its own preserve. A 1905 scheme for an Ackworth & Immingham Light Railway was successfully beaten off by the GCR to frustrate L & Y attempts to penetrate the area, even though the L & Y already had some presence there by means of the Axholme Joint Railway. The activities of the Yorkshire Light Railway Syndicate in various competing schemes of the period may be the reason why the Brackenhill Light Railway took so long to come into existence. There were two principal sources of traffic; coal and coke from Hemsworth Colliery, and stone from the quarries in the vicinity of Ackworth Moor Top; indeed, the quarry owners were involved in the negotiations for the building of the line and were at this time producing a large tonnage of high-quality grindstones. The BLR was eventually opened on 1 July 1914, though rather inauspiciously by all accounts. Although it was nominally an independent undertaking it was worked from the outset by the North Eastern Railway with two daily goods trains between the branch and Gascoigne Wood marshalling yards; some intermediate shunting was undertaken at Pontefract. The Midland Railway who appeared to be the dominant partner in the S & K appears to have had little interest in BLR and coal traffic destined for the Midland system was generally worked from Pontefract after the NE train had detached it in the sidings there. The centre of operations on the BLR was Ackworth Moor Top Goods Station where a relief clerk acted as Station Master and was assisted by one goods porter; one signalman at Brackenhill Junction and a goods guard completed the staffing of the line. On the first day of operation the relief clerk was dismayed to find the office at Moor Top in a dirty and disorganized state and he appears to have complained of the lack of stores necessary for the efficient running of the branch. Arrangements were actually made for a workmen's passenger service to be run over the line from Pontefract to Hemsworth Colliery halt with a stop at Moor Top when necessary but this never came to fruition. Although a Light

Railway, large NE locomotives were allowed on the branch and Class 'T' 0-8-0s were permitted to work a maximum load of 715 tons off the branch under the heading of Class C minerals. In later years the 'Q6's and 'B16's of Selby shed were the most common sight but almost any suitable available locomotive could be used, and when Selby shed closed, the final couple of years produced various locomotives from York. In its heyday the goods station at Moor Top did more business than the good yard on the main line at Ackworth but, as time went by one train per day was generally sufficient to serve the needs of the branch, as coal traffic had an alternative outlet on to the GN/GC system at Fitzwilliam. The Brackenhill Light Railway was officially closed on 1 January 1962 but before this the goods station at Moor Top was used as a bitumen depot. After closure it continued in use as a civil engineering contractor's yard, which function it still fulfills.

The final two stations on the GNR main line which came into the area were Hemsworth and South Elmsall. Both were built in the "Dutch" style of the WR & G, although Hemsworth was later re-built as an island platform station. Hemsworth closed in 1967 but South Elmsall remains as a good source of commuter traffic for Doncaster and Leeds. An unusual feature of the latter is that the exit from the platform into the booking office is below platform level. At Moorthorpe, just north of South Elmsall, junctions were made in both up and down directions with the Swinton & Knottingley Joint line which crossed over the GNR. In recent years this enabled trains which normally used the Midland main line, to travel from Leeds via Westgate down to the junction, onto the S & K and, finally, to re-join the Midland at Swinton. The S & KJ is discussed in a separate section of this book.

Today, the GNR line is the haunt of Inter-City 125's and dmu's with some occasional freight and locomotive hauled trains. The GC/Midland goods yard at Westgate is now the distribution centre for Ford cars and this has created the regular working into Westgate of car transporter trains.

The Hull and Barnsley Railway does not figure very largely in the railways of the Wakefield area but its main line (now lifted)

Ex-GNR Class 'C1' 4-4-2 No 4419 sets off from Westgate with the up 'West Riding Pullman'. The steam under the cab is from the booster which was fitted to the trailing axle in 1923. Other Modifications undertaken at the same time included LNER boiler mountings and a 'Pacific' type cab. The booster was removed in later years. Although the date of the photograph is unknown, it is almost certainly between 1923 and 1928 as livery changes took place after that period. The Pullman coaches are interesting as they carry the original livery with the cream panel extending up to the roof line and are mounted on American style six wheel bogies.
WAKEFIELD RAILWAY MODELLERS SOCIETY COLLECTION

passed through the southern part of the district and therefore must be included in this survey. The North Eastern Railway had an effective monopoly of railway working into the port of Hull and even though other companies might negotiate running powers into Hull over N E lines it could only be by accepting the conditions laid down by the NER, and so it became increasingly felt by the traders of Hull that they were losing the benefits that competition might otherwise bestow. In addition, the problems of moving coal and general merchandise through the port were exacerbated by the antiquated dock system which was owned by the Hull Dock Company and which, by all accounts, they were unwilling to modernise. At a meeting in Hull in May 1879 the Hull & Barnsley Railway Company was formed and backed by the Corporation which agreed to sell the necessary land and to subscribe a substantial amount of capital. The original title was The Hull, Barnsley & West Riding Junction Railway & Dock Company which bore witness to the fact that, not only was a line from Hull to the South Yorkshire Coalfields envisaged, but a large new deep water dock was also to be built on the shore of the Humber. The bill received the Royal Assent in August 1880 and both the Alexandra Dock and the main line were opened in 1885, with public service starting on 27 July. The original cumbersome title was abbreviated to the Hull & Barnsley Railway in 1905.

The Railway was principally a coal-carrying line and this traffic, of course was supplemented by general freight; but the passenger services never amounted to very much. The main line, such as it was, ran only from Hull to Cudworth where it ended in a one-platform terminal station adjacent to the Midland station; passengers for Barnsley had to change trains at Cudworth. As a passenger-carrying line it remained little more than a local branch line even though from 1905 a through service from Hull to Sheffield was put on by running over Midland lines from Cudworth to Sheffield. Most of the working of the H & B does not concern us here, but one interesting service which was instituted in the early years was a through working from Hull (Cannon Street) to Knottingley which gained the WP & G line at Hensall Junction. Although the service only lasted until

1912 it provided the through trains to Hull which the L & Y did not provide (L & Y expresses did not stop at Knottingley) and passengers for Hull via the L & Y route generally had to change at Goole. Had the major rebuilding of 1903 taken place at Pontefract Monkhill, the H & B service would have terminated there, thus making three separate routes by which passengers could have travelled from Pontefract to Hull. As things were, it was still possible to travel by these routes but changes at Knottingley or Goole were necessary for the H & B and L & Y routes but some through services were available from the S & K station. Apart from regular passenger services, the spur at Hensall Junction enabled special trains to run over the L & Y metals to Leeds via the Methley branch, and to Wakefield over the main line of the WP & G. H & B locomotives even penetrated into Lancashire on occasions. More importantly the spur was used by goods trains, and one night goods together with its return working took a H & B locomotive regularly to Whitham's sidings in Wakefield, making a stop at Pontefract en route in the early hours of the morning. The spur continued in use for the exchange of coal traffic at Hensall Junction sidings until the closure of the H & B line in 1959, but was later reopened to serve the new coal-fired power station at Drax; the branch is now extensively used by "merry-go-round" trains. Just within the Wakefield area was the most important junction outside of Hull, and this was situated at Wrangbrook (near Upton). It was, in effect, a double junction with a branch diverging from the main line to Wath-on-Dearne and another branch taking a sinuous course to Denaby via Pickburn and Sprotborough. Both of these were important coal-carrying lines though for a short while enjoyed passenger services. The Denaby branch was built first and opened for traffic in 1894; it was nominally an independent railway known as the South Yorkshire Junction Railway but was worked from the outset by the H & BR. The line tapped some of the newer collieries in the South Yorkshire coalfield area and was a source of lucrative traffic, but the severe gradients lying against loaded coal trains made it difficult to work. The passenger service was short-lived and finished in 1903; the trains actually ran from Denaby to

This view from Westgate footbridge was taken looking south with Class 'A1' 4-6-2 No 60128 *Bongrace* coming off the '99 arches' with the 1.20pm Kings Cross–Leeds in July 1962. The train was entering the down platform where a stop was made and any carriages for Bradford were detached by the station pilot.
R HEPWORTH

Carlton for operating convenience and to connect with services to Knottingley.

The Wath branch opened in 1902 and ran southwards to a small terminus at Wath just north of the GC station but made no physical connection, although it made connection by short branches to some important collieries: notably Frickley and Hickleton. As with the Denaby branch, coal trains had a good deal of heavy work to do to gain the main line at Wrangbrook. The passenger service on the Wath branch was rather more successful and lasted until 1929 with trains running between the terminus at Wath and Kirk Smeaton on the main line. The Wath branch served a station which just comes within the present Wakefield area and was situated at Moorhouse, just outside the town of South Elmsall. From Moorhouse (H & B) a branch made connection with the WR & G at Moorhouse Junction in an easterly direction and was built by the latter company. At the Wrangbrook end of the Wath branch a substantial yard was laid out with numerous sidings on both sides of the line where coal trains from both branches were marshalled for forwarding to Hull. Locomotive facilities provided at Wrangbrook included a turntable and water-softening plant. Stations were also provided on the main line at Upton & North Elmsall a little over a mile from Wrangbrook, and also at Hemsworth. Although the main line passenger service ceased at the beginning of 1932 the station at Upton remained open as a coal office until closure of the line, but Hemsworth, being rather far out of the town and not directly connected with a colliery (although geographically near to South Kirkby Colliery) was partly demolished. A useful spur was built by the H & B to link the main line at Hemsworth East Junction with the WR & G line in a northerly direction about a mile south of Hemsworth (WR & G) station: by this means coal could be drawn off the collieries situated on the WR & G line and worked to Hull. One further branch was planned to link the H & B near Hemsworth East Junction (running from east to south) to join the S & K line at Moorthorpe North Junction; the branch appears actually to have been built but it is thought that the points were never inserted at the junctions so that it carried no traffic and was later abandoned – had it been brought into use the Hull–Sheffield service mentioned previously could have been worked by this route. Today very little remains to remind us of the existence of the old H & B, but by its many tentacles spreading out from Wrangbrook Junction into the colliery districts of South Yorkshire, it played a full part in the transportation of coal for shipment from Hull. Much of this passed through the southern part of the Wakefield area before plunging into the murkiness of Barnsdale tunnel and emerging from the darkness into the rural acres of south east Yorkshire bound for Hull.

Class 'A3' 4-6-2 No 60061 *Pretty Polly* gets some young spotters excited as it travels light on the up line at Walton (south of Westgate). Above the locomotive can be seen the embankment of the St Pancras to Leeds line. This was a popular spot for local enthusiasts as it was possible to see trains on both lines.

R HEPWORTH

Sometime during late spring 1961 Class '5' 4-6-0 No 45434 of Willesden shed (1A) heads south through Walton station on the fast line of the former MR Normanton–Sheffield route, with a Class 'C' mixed goods. Note the unusual timber planked edge to the platform. The slow lines were routed along the right hand side of the station building and were fenced off from the general public.   R HEPWORTH

Just south of Walton station is a footbridge carrying a right of way over the railway. Class '6P' 4-6-0 No 45504 *Royal Signals* leaves the bridge as it travels the one time Midland route north with the down 'Devonian'. Note the typical Midland style double telegraph posts.
R HEPWORTH

Fowler Class '4F' 0-6-0 No 44274 about to head under the Wakefield to Doncaster road bridge as it passes Oakenshaw North Junction box with a rake of empty coal hoppers on 14 May 1960. The junction and the tracks to the right were installed by the LMS to make a connection with the Kirkgate to Goole line.   P COOKSON

Normanton station in the very early days of the North Midland Railway. The lithograph shows the view looking towards Altofts Junction.
                                                                      CITY OF WAKEFIELD MD ARCHIVES GOODCHILD LOAN MSS

An L&Y 4-4-0 forms the background to this group photograph of some of the engine shed personnel at Normanton probably taken arounds the turn of the century.
CITY OF WAKEFIELD MD ARCHIVES GOODCHILD LOAN MSS

Ex-Midland Railway Class '2F' No 3758 is turned on the station yard turntable at Normanton on 29 June 1933. Locomotives arriving with trains from Lancashire were usually turned in the yard instead of using the shed facilities. Although ten years after Amalgamation No 3758 still retains the early LMS livery.
H C CASSERLEY

A visitor from the north east in the shape of Class 'V2' 2-6-2 No 60809 *The Snapper* runs tender first onto Normanton shed in 1964.
R ROCKETT

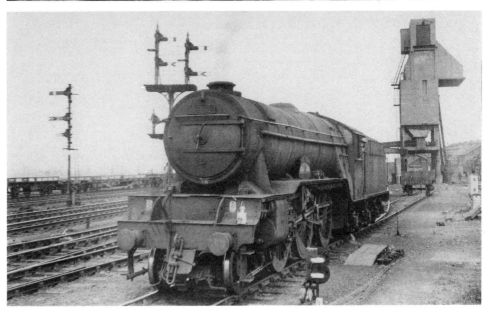

To the north of Royston was Royston Junction where the Thornhill branch left the Midland main line. Running tender first Class '8F' 2-8-0 No 48222 approaches the junction with an up train of empty mineral wagons. The bracket signals on the right control the exit from the branch which can be seen in the right-hand corner of the photograph.
J E FARLINE

Looking towards Royston Junction from Middlestown station on the Thornhill Branch in May 1963. The station was used for goods traffic only.
R HEPWORTH

This photograph shows the junction at Middlestown where a spur left the Midland Railway Thornhill branch to join the L&Y at Healey Mills. The double track branch carried on past the signal cabin to Thornhill and, eventually, Dewsbury.
G HALLOS COLLECTION

The Great Central Railway had a line from just north of Nostell to Barnsley. This November 1961 photograph shows the point where the GC was crossed at a higher level by the L&Y. The GC line continued into the distance to Wintersett & Ryhill station, then on to Barnsley. The L&Y from Wakefield (to the right), continued to Ryhill Halt and eventually joined the Dearne Valley Railway at Shafton.

R WALKER

LNER Class 'J39' 0-6-0 No 64763 at Long Dams as it approaches Wintersett & Ryhill station with a train of empty mineral wagons from Ardsley yard to South Yorkshire.

R WALKER

Wintersett & Ryhill during the early part of this century. The road bridge in the background is still in existence and carries the present Station Road. The far side platform can also still be seen although now very much overgrown.　　　　GCR SOCIETY

Returning now to the GNR main line, a 'WD' 2-8-0 heads south through Nostell with a coal train. Although the station building was still intact when photographed in July 1963 the footbridge, platforms and other effects have all disappeared. In the far distance was the triangular junction onto the GC line to Barnsley.　　　　R HEPWORTH

Hemsworth station was originally built in the same style as the other WR&G stations but in 1912 when the line was widened it was rebuilt as an island platform. In this 1948 photograph Class 'A3' 4-6-2 No 56 *Centenary* heads a Leeds–Doncaster slow.   R HOLLIDAY

A short freight from the North Lincolnshire area heads north past South Elmsall goods yard in 1957 behind Class '04/7' No 63616 of Immingham Shed. Although the line was built by the GN and GC Companies, most of the traffic came off the GN at Doncaster.

P COOKSON

An unidentified Class '8F' propels a couple of brake vans off the South Yorkshire Junction Line (Denaby branch) and heads towards Wrangbrook Junction. The Wath branch can be seen over the banking to the right. The photograph was taken one September afternoon during a visit to the Wrangbrook area.
P COOKSON

A coal train is shown pulling out of the sidings at Upton Colliery and crossing to the main line through the station. The colliery, which encountered severe geological problems, is now closed and virtually all traces of this scene have disappeared. The locomotive is former WD 2-8-0 No 90488 and was photographed in 1962 after the main line to the east of Wrangbrook had been closed. P COOKSON

The Wath branch looking towards Wrangbrook Junction and showing a WD 2-8-0 pulling out of the sidings with an eastbound coal train. The old H&B signals on substantial wooden posts will be noted (1957).   P COOKSON

The West yard on the Wath branch at Wrangbrook looking south. On the sky-line can be seen the water-softening plant for the locomotive water-supply, and on the right a WD 2-8-0 is on the turntable before setting out with a coal train for Hull (1957). P COOKSON

4 | The Swinton & Knottingley Joint

The Swinton & Knottingley Joint Railway owes its existence to the fact that in the second half of the 19th century Normanton was proving to be a very serious bottle-neck in the flow of traffic from the Midlands to the North East, most of which was exchanged at the station or at the adjacent goods yards, and, in spite of the rebuilding of 1867/8 the problem still remained a serious one. As mentioned in the section on the WP & G, the opening of the direct NE route from Doncaster to York via Selby in 1871 took most of the Doncaster–York traffic away from the N E Knottingley to Burton Salmon branch so that it was by this time only lightly used. T E Harrison (of the NER) suggested to James Allport (of the MR) that the construction of a short line from Ferrybridge on the NE to a point near Swinton on the MR would effect a direct route between Sheffield and York which avoided the congested stretch of line through Normanton. This suggestion was taken up and the two companies deposited a bill early in 1874. However, at the same time a similar but competing bill known as the Leeds, Pontefract & Sheffield Junction Railway was submitted by the GNR and MS & LR. This was to cover almost the same route but would have differed at the northern end by including a branch to the L & Y at Knottingley in addition to the junction with the NE at Ferrybridge. The MR and NER argued that such a scheme was no concern of other companies and that the project was simply one to improve the flow of traffic from the Midland to the North Eastern and was therefore the proper concern of themselves alone. The GNR and MS & LR argued that they were desiring to build a line which would be available to all interested companies to use on fair terms. The resulting Parliamentary contest ended in stalemate with both schemes being rejected. However, it appears that differences were soon resolved and the MR/NER bill was quickly re-committed with running powers over the line inserted for the GNR and MS & LR, and in this form the Act was secured in July 1874. The length of the main line is about 15½ miles and it shortened the old Sheffield–York route via Normanton by about 13 miles. There were to be four branch connections to the railway. The first one lay outside the Wakefield area but was to provide a most important link between the MS & L at Mexborough and the S & K at Dearne Junction; in later years (after the MS & L had become the Great Central Railway) it was used by a large number of cross country services using the GC route to the south. The other three branches all came within the present Wakefield area; two were constructed in the vicinity of Moorthorpe to connect with the West Riding & Grimsby line: the first from Moorthorpe station to South Kirkby Junction taking a generally north-westerly direction, and the second from Moorthorpe North Junction to South Elmsall station in a generally south-easterly direction. The fourth branch was in Pontefract and consisted of a loop line round the eastern side of the town taking a northerly exit from the S & K station (Baghill) and coming into the L & Y station (Monkhill) from the east. A further branch which was to prove very useful was built a little later at the southern end of the line as a joint venture by the MS & L and the MR/NER, and this was a westerly connection from the S & K to the MS & L at Wath. The line was eventually completed and opened for passenger traffic in July 1879, goods and mineral traffic having been started a little earlier (which was often the case). There are no engineering features of special note though the terrain is quite hilly and cuttings and embankments abound; however, there is a substantial viaduct over the valley of the River Went to the south of Ackworth station. The most severe gradient is 1 in 150 which could be quite testing for heavy trains and the writer can remember many instances of good trains having been signal-checked at Ferrybridge and then facing a stiff climb of a couple of miles or so to the other side of Pontefract from a standing start – to witness a Class 'B16' 4-6-0 tackling this was well worth seeing!

There were many instances of the joint nature of the line: signals and signal boxes for example were all pure NE from Ferrybridge to Moorthorpe North, but from the station box at Moorthorpe to the South, the pattern was Midland. In such things as letter headings, tickets, uniforms, waiting room seats etc., the styles S & K Jt or M & NE were adopted. The stations however were all of a pattern, with the main building made up of three blocks forming (in plan) a horizontally elongated 'H', and all situated on the down side – or was it the up side? One of the problems in the use of the terms up and down on the S & K was that for the Midland, Up implied to the south (i.e. towards Sheffield, Derby and St Pancras) while for the North Eastern, Up implied to the north (i.e. to York). Although all were built to the same basic plan, Pontefract (Baghill) was larger than the others and had five platforms: two through with a bay on the south side, and two bay platforms at the northern end formed effectively, a terminus of the branch from Monkhill. Oddly, there were no footbridges on S & K stations and the lines were crossed on the level by the usual wooden sleepers, except at Pontefract where a subway was provided.

At the opening of the line the passenger service was run by the Midland Railway and Midland locomotives were stationed at York for both passenger and freight workings, the North Eastern Railway appearing to be content to allow other companies to run their trains into York. A little later, the introduction of a short-lived working from Milford Junction to Hull, also by the Midland Railway, gave a service to Hull from the S & K line. At first the main line service appeared to be of a local nature with some through coaches from the north east being attached at Sheffield to the principal Bradford–Bristol trains, but as time went by Newcastle–Bristol trains ran independently in their own right. The Great Northern Railway began to exercise its running powers over the S & K by instituting a service from Doncaster to York via Ackworth and Pontefract, using the branch from South Elmsall to Moorthorpe North Junction, which incidentally, made a third route by which GN trains travelled from Doncaster to York (the other two being via Selby and Knottingley). This was short-lived however and disappeared during wartime economy cuts in 1917. The South Elmsall–Moorthorpe curve continued in use for freight trains until the LNER era when it was closed in 1928. Upon the opening of the Pontefract loop line in April 1880, the North Eastern Railway itself began to run trains into Baghill, but from Leeds (New) station by a rather round-about route via Garforth, Kippax, Castleford (NE) and Pontefract (Monkhill). This route made use of the Leeds, Castleford & Pontefract Junction Railway as far as Cutsyke Junction and then the L & Y line from that point to Pontefract East Junction before gaining the S & K branch to Baghill. This was a useful service in its day which supplemented rather than competed with the more direct service to Leeds (Wellington) from the L & Y station.

It is relevant to digress a little from the main account at this point. It is to be expected that there would be a good deal of passenger traffic between two towns as closely situated as Pontefract and Castleford and so long as there was no other competition, the railways could be expected to carry the bulk of

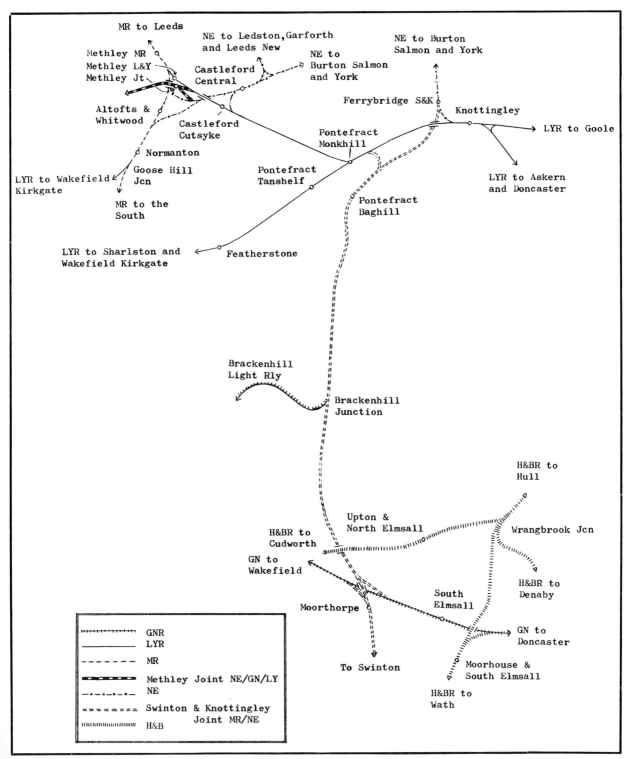

MR to Leeds

NE to Ledston, Garforth
and Leeds New

NE to Burton
Salmon and York

Methley MR
Methley L&Y
Methley Jt

Castleford
Central

NE to
Burton Salmon
and York

Ferrybridge S&K

Knottingley

Altofts &
Whitwood

Castleford
Cutsyke

LYR to Goole

Normanton

Pontefract
Monkhill

LYR to Wakefield
Kirkgate

Goose Hill
Jcn

Pontefract
Tanshelf

LYR to Askern
and Doncaster

MR to the
South

Pontefract
Baghill

LYR to Sharlston and
Wakefield Kirkgate

Featherstone

Brackenhill
Light Rly

Brackenhill
Junction

H&BR to
Hull

Upton &
North Elmsall

Wrangbrook Jcn

H&BR to
Cudworth

GN to
Wakefield

H&BR to
Denaby

South
Elmsall

GN to
Doncaster

Moorthorpe

To Swinton

Moorhouse &
South Elmsall

H&BR to
Wath

	GNR
	LYR
	MR
	Methley Joint NE/GN/LY
	NE
	Swinton & Knottingley Joint MR/NE
	H&B

it; but, as with many other areas, the turn of the century saw the introduction of urban electric tramways and the Pontefract, Castleford and Normanton line of the West Riding Electric Tramways connected the towns from centre to centre with frequent tramcar services. Although the Leeds–Baghill railway service survived until 1926 much of the local traffic had been taken by the trams and the Castleford–Pontefract section closed

to regular passengers, though the Castleford to Leeds (NE) service survived until 1951. The route however remained open for goods and special traffic, and even into the 1960s excursion trains were run over it from Kippax to Cleethorpes.

The fourth company to make extensive use of the S & K line was the MS & LR though at first only over the Southern part of it on a regular basis. For a few years from 1879, the MS & L put on a service of trains from Sheffield (Victoria) to Leeds (Central) using the S & K as far as Moorthorpe but then running on to the WR & G line by means of the branch to South Kirkby, and reaching Leeds via Wakefield (Westgate). This service which competed with the Sheffield–Leeds service of the Midland Railway lasted only until 1893. It was with the opening of the London extension of the MS & LR (in 1899) and the change of title to the Great Central Railway, that the greatest variety of through expresses began to use the S & K line. Although the Sheffield–Leeds service was resuscitated for a while from 1903, the main trains began to run through from York and Newcastle to such destinations as Nottingham, Leicester, Oxford, Southampton, Bournemouth and various destinations in South Wales via the Woodford to Banbury line. Many of these trains eventually stopped at Pontefract. GCR freight traffic did not generally work through to York in the early years but was handed over to the NER at Milford Junction. A fifth Company working into Pontefract S & K was the L & YR but this traffic was generally limited to transfer goods from the yard at Monkhill. Thus, by the turn of the century the S & K line was being used by a great variety of services, the majority of which stopped at Pontefract. Other trains which made use of the line were those from Hull to Pontefract which connected with main line trains to and from the Midland and GC routes to the South. One special source of passenger traffic to Pontefract S & K station ought to be mentioned. As the town had become established as a garrison, large numbers of military personnel travelled to and from the Barracks during both world wars, and most of them came via Baghill station. There are many men all over the country who know Pontefract because they were "stationed" there during the war and whose first sight of the town would be Baghill Station. Another source of special traffic which benefited the Pontefract stations generally was race traffic which came to the town from all directions, though not all of it ran to Tanshelf station which was nearest to the race course. Perhaps the times of greatest activity on the S & K line were those peak summer Saturdays of the early 1950s when no freight ran and many of the main line trains were duplicated, in addition to which there were hosts of Saturdays Only workings from the Midlands to Bridlington, Filey and Scarborough. By the beginning of the 1960s much of this began to disappear as the pattern of family holidays changed with the greatly increased use of private cars and the growing popularity of continental holidays. Various other changes of the post-Beeching period had an impact on the S & K J, but one slight improvement of service occurred in January 1960 before a general decline set in. The Methley Joint Line service from Leeds Central to Castleford was extended to Baghill for which the loop line was relaid and resignalled at the end of 1959, but the service ceased in 1964 with the closure of the Methley Joint and the loop line was later taken up. Alterations to the junctions to the north of Sheffield and the closure of the Great Central main line saw the end of cross country services using this route and all S & K services which had used Sheffield Victoria were switched to the Midland station. Rationalization of railways in Leeds involving the closure of Leeds Central and the concentration of all passenger services at the rebuilt City station had the effect of introducing some extra trains to the southern end of the S & K line. By means of a new curve connecting City station with the GN line out of Leeds, trains for the Midlands and the South-West could run via Wakefield (Westgate) and gain the S & K line at Moorthorpe via South Kirkby Junction, in preference to the more direct route via Normanton. This took place in 1968 and lasted until 1973 when a much more fundamental change took place which is mentioned in the section on Castleford and the Y & NM line. The whole service of through expresses was removed from the S & K and put on to the Normanton lines; the move was not a success however, and at the time of writing they are all back on the S & K but are due to be taken off yet again so that by mid 1984 all that will remain of a once marvellously varied service will be six dmu's each way per day plying between Sheffield and York. A passenger service therefore remains precariously, but the proposed introduction of pay-trains to the line may see the end of manned stations in the near future. Freight traffic remains quite vigorous with a variety of through block loads and the inevitable "merry-go-round" trains serving the ever-hungry power stations.

A general view of Moorthorpe station looking south in 1960. The neat appearance of the well-kept station gardens will be noted. The Midland style signal box – Moorthorpe Station Junction – is just visible on the platform behind the waiting rooms.

P COOKSON

A northbound fast goods train at Brackenhill Junction (on the S&KJ) hauled by 'B1' 4-6-0 No 61122 about 1960. The signals at this time were all wooden slotted arm types of NE origin and the Brackenhill branch can be seen curving to the right on its way to Moor Top and Hemsworth Colliery.   P COOKSON

The rather chaotic site of Moor Top goods station in 1960. Nothing remains of the goods station itself but a reminder of NE days still existed in the form of an old wooden fixed-distant signal, and the branch was still open for coal traffic from Hemsworth colliery.   P COOKSON

Class 'Q6' No 63387 is being re-railed at the entrance to the Goods Yard at Baghill station, Pontefract about 1950. In all probability the locomotive had been shunting coal into the sidings (having worked from the Brackenhill branch) and ran foul of the points on returning to the main line. The method of lifting by means of the holes in the front of the locomotive main frames can be clearly seen.   P TAIT

Opposite top: Ackworth station was closed to regular passengers in 1951 but stayed open for special traffic. Although now demolished, the goods shed still stands rather forlornly and has seen no sidings there for nearly 30 years. The train is a 1961 Whit-Monday excursion to Scarborough via the S&KJ, headed by 'K3' class 2-6-0 No 61883.   P COOKSON

Opposite bottom: One of the services which ran via Sheffield Victoria and the GC main line was the Newcastle/York–Swansea train seen here leaving Pontefract on a hot June day in 1957 behind Class 'D11' 4-4-0 No 62666 *Zeebrugge*.   P COOKSON

A view looking south from the end of Pontefract Baghill platform. The main goods shed is visible in the centre background and the goods offices were integral with it. A subsidiary wooden shed for malt traffic can be seen behind the brake-van on the right. The photograph was taken on a Saturday afternoon in 1956 when the sidings were full of coal and coke traffic which had earlier come in off the Brackenhill branch and two 4Fs had been sent down from Canklow (Rotherham) to remove it. The locomotive (No 44111) in the south bay platform has already turned on the turntable and sister engine No 44477 is running wrong line to the top end of the yard to turn also. After the passage of the Newcastle–Bristol train in the mid-afternoon the two trains would make their way south.   P COOKSON

This view of a MR delivery dray shows a number of interesting features. The weigh office is visible behind the cart and in the horsedock a horsebox and a well-limed cattle truck are standing. It was to be some 20 years before the hill behind Baghill station was to be covered by housing and at this time the station was very much on the edge of the town.
MAUD PHOTOGRAPHY, PONTEFRACT

Opposite top: The pull out of Pontefract (S&K) offered the chance of good smoke effects though it is remarkable how frequently heavy trains were hauled away from the station with the locomotive showing a clear chimney. However, on this murky January day in 1961 Patriot No 45519 *Lady Godiva* obliged with quite a good show.   P COOKSON

Opposite bottom: A Newcastle–Birmingham express draws into Pontefract Baghill in the summer of 1958. Double-headers were quite common on the S&K, but this was as much for operating convenience as for extra locomotive power. The leading Class '5' is No 44813.   P COOKSON

The LMS Beyer Garratt's were daily visitors to the S&K line on iron ore trains to the Tees-side area or, sometimes, on coal trains to York. Along with No 47978 the Garratt's used were almost always those based at Hasland (Chesterfield) and only infrequently those from Toton. On one occasion the writer remembers one of these huge locomotives being sent down to shunt the yard at Pontefract instead of the usual '4F'. Note the mile-post which reads 14 miles to Wath Road Junction. Photograph taken in 1955.   P COOKSON

Baghill (or Bag Hill as it used to be known) was an elevated site from which a good view of Pontefract could be commanded and it appears to have been popular with the producers of early view-cards. There are at least five different photographs of this view from the Edwardian era which include the station as foreground. This one shows the main building together with Station Lane, the subway, and a little of the two bay platforms at the northern end. As the station was built on a curve it was never possible to obtain a good view of the whole of it.   P COOKSON COLLECTION

The Pontefract loop line was never very extensively used but such trains as did use it were often interesting excursions or specials of one sort or another. One regular excursion which ran for a number of years in the 1950s started at Kippax and ran via Castleford and Pontefract to Cleethorpes hauled by a Leeds Neville Hill locomotive. The train here, shown about 1956, is hauled by Class 'B16' 4-6-0 No 61429 and is making its way slowly round the branch which had been singled but not relaid; it is crossing the viaduct over Knottingley Road. P COOKSON

The loop was later relaid as a single line for the introduction of the Leeds (Central)–Baghill dmu service, and the photograph shows Class '5' No 44688 coming from the Baghill end with a race-train bound for Tanshelf. Race trains were about the only ones which would travel through all three Pontefract Stations. The photograph was taken in 1961. P COOKSON

Ex NER Class 'J27' 0-6-0 No 65881 was seen in 1958 heading north on a freight train near to Ferrybridge signal box just before crossing the River Aire. The train has probably come round the curve from Knottingley and is on the NE branch to Burton Salmon and destined for Gascoigne Wood Yard.   P TAIT

The northern end of the S&K Joint line is shown in this 1956 picture of 'B16' No 61460 heading south on a York–Mexborough freight. At this date the Ferrybridge Signal box was situated in the V between the NE and S&K lines but was later removed to a point north of the station to be nearer the power station complex.
P COOKSON

Up to the establishment of Goole as a port for foreign trade in 1827, the place was little more than a hamlet, but the building of the Knottingley and Goole canal and various dock works at Goole by the Aire & Calder Navigation Company, led to the town's quick development as an inland port and its desirability for railway connection.

The Wakefield, Pontefract & Goole Railway was the successful one of four schemes which were put before Parliament in the session of 1845: but only after a hard fought contest. The defeated schemes were the Barnsley & Goole, the Doncaster & Goole (or Goole & Doncaster) and the Brayton & Goole (a Hudson Y & NM Company). The Board of Trade report found that the first two schemes were too much dependent on the export of coal from South Yorkshire, and the last one, even though it was backed by Hudson's forceful personality, and would have been cheaper to build, was considered to make too circuitous a route from Goole to the hinterland. There was actually one further minor scheme put forward at the same time which was proposed by the Canal Company: for a short line from Goole to Snaith, but this was rejected very quickly on account of its conferring a monopoly of trading on the Canal Company.

The WP & G Company was launched at a meeting in Pontefract Town Hall in September 1844 at which two local gentlemen, George Fox and William Moxon were appointed to draw up plans and sections which were successively presented to the London & York Company, the Direct Northern Company, and the York & North Midland for their assistance, but the scheme was rejected by all three. However, after an approach to the Manchester & Leeds Railway it was successfully taken up by Captain Laws on its behalf, with the M & L agreeing to subscribe half the capital and appointing five directors, and the WP & G doing likewise. The Act of Incorporation allowed for the amalgamation of the two companies, and this was eventually agreed at the end of 1845. By the Act which confirmed this amalgamation in 1847, the Manchester & Leeds became the Lancashire & Yorkshire Railway with the WP & G line becoming its outlet to the east. A large-scale map of the proposed line, in Pontefract Museum, shows a proposed branch from a point near Crofton to the NMR at Oakenshaw, and a branch at Goole (at about the point of the junction later known as Goole West) which ran to the staith at Shuffleton Bight. The most remarkable feature however, was a complex system of junctions near to the village of Gowdall where the WP & G was due to cross the London & York main line: here all possible connections were to be made – North to East, East to South, South to West, and West to North; the appearance on the map being that of a four-pointed star. Also marked on the same map is the proposed Doncaster–Wakefield branch of the London & York meeting the WP & G almost exactly in the same way and at the same place as the later Dearne Valley line at Crofton West Junction. The map is signed by John Harris (who was appointed resident engineer) and dated 30 November 1844 although it is acknowledged as having been received by the Clerk of the Peace for the Borough of Pontefract at 8.30pm on November 3th. In the event, the Crofton to Oakenshaw North Junction branch was not built until very much later – by the LMS in fact, and opened in 1928. The London and York Railway (later known as the Great Northern Railway) endured some years of very fierce struggle for survival and when it was eventually completed as a main line from London to York had lost the Doncaster to

Wakefield branch and the line to York terminated in the famous "ploughed field" near Askern. Connection was, however, effected between the GNR and Wakefield and Leeds by means of two branches incorporated in an Act of 1846. One of these (a projection of William Moxon) was to strike South East from Knottingley through Womersley, Norton and Askern to make an end-on junction with the GNR just beyond Askern. At this time the village of Askern was noted for the medicinal properties of its waters and, had history taken a different turn, it might well have become a fashionable Spa, but in the event, with the sinking of Askern Main Colliery in later years it became a small mining town. In addition to general agricultural produce the line was expected to carry a large amount of limestone, the quarrying of which centred on the village of Womersley. The second branch was to strike North West from Pontefract to meet the North Midland line at Methley Junction passing through Castleford (at Cutsyke) on the way; the L & Y station at Methley was situated on the curve just before the junction. The North Midland station was some three-quarters of a mile north of the junction and became known as Methley North in later years. The station on the Methley Joint Line (known as Methley South in recent times) was the third in this small but straggling village. (We add here that, although Methley is not actually in the Wakefield Metropolitan area, it is so inextricably bound up with the railway development of the district that it cannot be omitted). Thus, with the opening of these two branches, Pontefract and Knottingley were situated at the centre of an intersection of two important secondary lines of the L & YR.

The main WP & G line opened for public service on 1 April 1848 to great festivity, while the Askern branch opened a little later, but through working into Doncaster was not possible until the GNR completed its line in September of that year. Because of financial restrictions the Methley branch was another year before completion but it was finished just in time for race traffic to run from Leeds to Doncaster for the St Leger meeting of 1849. Connection had now been made between the GN system and Wakefield by means of the L & YR, and between the GN system and Leeds by the L & YR as far as Methley and by the North Midland line thence to Leeds. One other short but very important line needs now to be mentioned: the Y & NM branch from Burton Salmon to Knottingley which is a little less than three miles long. When Hudson realized that the GNR (London & York) would survive in spite of his strenuous efforts to kill it, and would provide a much more direct route from London to York than the older route using the Midland Railway and the York & North Midland Railway (of which he was in charge), he decided to cut his losses and allow the GN running powers into York over his own line, which meant that the Burton Salmon–Knottingley link had to be built to make this possible, and an Act for this was obtained in 1847. This move enabled Hudson to exercise some control over the GNR entry into York, while the GNR was able to save expense on the construction of its own independent line from Askern to York. Because of engineering difficulties encountered in the building of a tubular design of bridge over the river Aire at Ferrybridge, the line was not opened fully until 1850.

Although the GN main line was not yet in its final form, an East Coast Route was now available from London to York and the North, though by means of the L & YR and Y & NM systems between Doncaster and York. Over the next few years Knottingley outgrew Pontefract in railway importance because of its situation on the East Coast Route, and it was not until 1871 when the North Eastern line from Shaftholme Junction (near Askern) to York, via Selby was built, that main line trains took a more direct route from Doncaster to York. During this period of Knottingley's importance as a railway centre it became necessary to enlarge the station and powers were obtained to construct a new station at joint GN and L & Y expense. The new depot completed in 1854 had five platforms and an overall roof and was established as the place for changing trains for different destinations. With the opening of the Bradford, Wakefield & Leeds Railway from Wakefield to Leeds in 1857, GNR trains from Doncaster and the south were diverted from the Methley branch to run via Wakefield into Leeds Central station which had become the terminus for the GNR. L & YR local trains continued to run from Leeds Wellington to Doncaster via the original Methley route. The late E L Ahrons who wrote extensively (and often wittily) about train services in the latter part of last century, gives some interesting insights into the L & YR of the period describing it as probably the most degenerate railway in the kingdom – a railway of ugly and inconvenient stations, of deplorable unpunctuality in the running of trains, and with rolling stock which seemed to be falling apart. During the 1860s the L & YR began to wake up to the fact that the GNR was steadily building up its own empire in West Yorkshire in areas that might be regarded as L & Y territory, and in an effort to secure an outlet for its traffic to the south, independent of the GNR, the L & Y entered into an agreement with the Great Eastern Railway in 1864 to build a line from Askern L & Y to link up with the GE main line near Cambridge and so gain access to London at Liverpool Street. The scheme envisaged both parties contributing equally to this very substantial undertaking and each enjoying running powers over the lines of the other Company. The bill was eventually defeated (the GNR strenuously opposing it) and this interesting might-have-been never came to fruition.

Another scheme which did materialise and was to have a considerable effect on the WP & G section of the L & YR also concerned the GNR, this time in league with the Manchester, Sheffield & Lincolnshire Railway. This was the joint line known as the West Riding & Grimsby Railway opened in 1866 and linking Doncaster with Wakefield (Westgate) via South Elmsall. This is dealt with more fully in the section dealing with Wakefield (Westgate) and it is sufficient here to note that its effect on the WP & G was to remove most of the GN traffic between Doncaster, Wakefield and Leeds from the L & Y lines through Knottingley and Pontefract. The opening of the main direct North Eastern route from York to Shaftholme Junction in 1871 also removed most of the GN traffic from the Knottingley–Burton Salmon route, thereby completing the reduction in status of the Pontefract and Knottingley area as part of the East Coast Main Line. It should however be mentioned that the Knottingley route continued to be used by some East Coast route trains, particularly those from Kings Cross to Harrogate which ran via Church Fenton to avoid reversal at Leeds Central and also by some freight trains. In addition, to the present day, L & Y lines are used as diversionary routes whenever the WR & G or the main York line are closed for engineering work. Although through passenger traffic fell away after these developments the lines were still very busy with local passenger traffic and principally with freight. Up to the opening of the NE from Thorne to Staddlethorpe in 1869 with its branch to the WP & G at Goole, L & Y passenger trains terminated at Goole, but the opening of the new NE station in the town together with the new branch, made it physically possible for L & Y trains to use the North Eastern Station and also to gain direct access to Hull. The year 1870 then saw the L & Y take advantage of this and the Goole branch began to accommodate through expresses from Liverpool and Manchester to Hull; during this period the L & YR became established in Hull and many through freight trains were run to and from that city. Eric Mason, who was a much

respected authority on L & Y matters, mentions four of the heaviest through goods trains operated by the L & Y in the early years of the present century and three of these were night trains using the WP & G line to Goole and Hull. The services from Liverpool to Hull were generally worked in the same train as those to York with the Hull coaches being detached at Wakefield (Kirkgate) and then working non-stop to Goole, so that Pontefract and Knottingley did not actually enjoy the benefit of these services directly.

Just after the turn of the century in 1903, another scheme of local interest was proposed. Presumably the L & Y were to acknowledge the status of Pontefract as the principal town along the WP & G line because it was announced that the incommodious station at Monkhill was to be rebuilt, but as a much bigger station some hundred yards to the west, which would place it in the Vee formed by the Wakefield and Methley lines; a new approach road was to be built, the station was to have bay platforms in addition to through platforms, and it was also to have refreshment rooms. Freight facilities were to be much improved with the inclusion of many additional sidings and running loops. Evidently, from contemporary newspaper accounts, the Knottingley Depot was to be transferred to Pontefract together with the terminus of the Hull & Barnsley Railway service from Hull. All in all the scheme envisaged a station on quite a grand scale, though in the end no work was carried out on the project even though land from the Earlsmount Estate had been purchased for the purpose. It is interesting to note that at the same time a branch was proposed along the course of the later BR branch (opened in 1965) between the WP & G and Ferrybridge :NE) which would have enabled L & Y traffic bound for York to avoid Normanton by using the WP & G line from Wakefield and thence through Pontefract to Ferrybridge. It may have been that for financial reasons the scheme was not implemented because the early years of the twentieth century saw a large increase in the amount of coal traffic using local lines, to the extent that the L & Y Company had to undertake a number of local improvement schemes which included the provision of extra running lines and sidings at Featherstone, Knottingley and Whitley Bridge to accommodate the extra trains. Also, to facilitate the working of coal trains from the Askern Branch to Goole for shipping, a line was built and opened in 1915 from Knottingley South Junction to Knottingley Depot West to enable trains to work directly from south to east in order to avoid reversal at Knottingley station. It is relevant to mention here that the L & YR had a locomotive shed at Knottingley which was a sub-shed of Wakefield. Its duties consisted of local passenger and freight working in the area but, as L & Y locomotives were stationed at Wakefield, Goole, Leeds and Doncaster, its workings were found to be dispensable and it closed in 1922. There is little to be said about the other stations on the WP & G line which lie within the Wakefield area. At the opening of the line in 1848 Featherstone was the only one and it was built in the same style as most of the others – a rather elaborate cottage style. However, it was very conveniently situated along the main shopping street of the town and well patronized. Crofton and Sharlston were built rather later and Pontefract Tanshelf later still – about 1871. The first two were closed in 1931 and 1958 respectively but Tanshelf remained open until 1967 when along with Featherstone it was closed upon withdrawal of the Wakefield–Goole service. Tanshelf station was built to serve the western side of Pontefract and was nearer to the actual town centre than Monkhill which was situated nearer to the older part of the town in the vicinity of the Castle. It was also close by Pontefract race-course and the platforms appear to have been lengthened in order to accommodate excursion trains for the races; additionally, a bay platform was provided on the up side, presumably for the use of race trains, as no regular normal passenger trains appear to have started at Tanshelf. The station was also very convenient for the hundreds of miners using it daily for the journey to

Featherstone for Ackton Hall and Featherstone Main Collieries. Although the main goods yard was situated at Monkhill, Tanshelf still had the goods shed and sidings normally expected at a small station and was served by trip workings from Monkhill. Regrettably there appear to have been few photographs taken on the section between Crofton and Tanshelf.

The Knottingley–Doncaster section of the Leeds (City)–Doncaster LMS Service ceased in 1948, though the 1946 Bradshaw shows but a single train from Askern to Leeds in the morning with a corresponding return in the evening. The Leeds–Knottingley and the Wakefield–Goole services remained until dieselization in March 1958 when the structure was altered to some extent. The Wakefield–Goole service was extended so that trains ran from Bradford or Wakefield to Goole or Hull, with some running through from Bradford to Hull; while the Leeds–Knottingley service was cut back to Pontefract (Monkhill) for some services and Monkhill was then regarded as the changing point for Goole and Hull. The beginning of 1960 saw the extension of the Leeds (Central–Castleford trains to Monkhill and thence to Baghill, but this was not successful because only off-peak trains ran through, leaving the main services of morning and evening to terminate at Castleford! The service ceased in November 1964 along with that of the whole of the Methley Joint Line. Leeds City–Knottingley trains continued to use the Methley (L & Y) branch until 1968. Meanwhile in 1967 the Wakefield–Goole service had been withdrawn and replaced by a Leeds–Goole working which, upon closure of the station at Cutsyke, was then re-routed via Castleford Central. This situation obtains at the time of writing but under the West Yorkshire PTE the Leeds–Goole service is under review in common with many others. At the present time the former WP & G lines are still quite busy, mainly with ''merry-go-round'' trains. The 1960s saw a period of expansion with the opening of Kellingley Colliery (to the east of Knottingley) and power stations at Ferrybridge, Eggborough, and Drax. To cope with this extra work a new Diesel Depot was opened at Knottingley and new branches at Ferrybridge and Eggborough were opened in 1965 and 1966 respectively. In contrast, the section beyond the reinstated branch at Hensall Junction sees little through traffic and has now been singled from Snaith to Goole. The WP & G lines may see more traffic in the near future as the opening of the new Selby coalfield is likely to bring much more ''merry-go-round'' traffic bound for Drax power station, and as modern mining techniques improve, the deeply-lying coal in the Snaith area may well be mined in the not-too-distant future to provide yet more coal trains.

At Pontefract East Junction the L&Y line is joined by the branch from the S&K at Baghill, seen trailing in on the right. At the time of this photograph (1960) it had been relaid as a single line and was used by the dmu's from Leeds Central to Baghill. The train coming up from Knottingley is a Bank Holiday excursion from Knottingley to Blackpool, hauled by Class '8F' 2-8-0 No 48506 which was one of several involved in tender exchanges with some of the 'Jubilee's' that had previously been paired with Fowler tenders.   P COOKSON

The Methley Junction end of the Pontefract–Methley branch is shown in this view of Class '8F' 2-8-0 No 48311 on an empty wagon train bound for Glasshoughton or Prince of Wales Colliery during the summer of 1960. The main building of the L&Y station is visible on the left and Methley Junction signal box is faintly visible in the background. It was normal practice for locomotives to work tender first towards Pontefract and chimney first with loaded coal trains for Hunslet Lane sidings.   P COOKSON

On the line from Wakefield Kirkgate to Pontefract and Goole was taken this circa 1910 view of Featherstone station looking east. The area was busy however, and warranted quadruple track between Featherstone and Streethouse to serve the coal traffic brought out from the collieries of the district. Ackton Hall and Sharlston collieries are now the only ones open, Snydale and Featherstone Main having since been closed.   P COOKSON COLLECTION

The other station on the L&Y line in Pontefract was situated about ¾ mile to the west of Monkhill and named Tanshelf after what was at one time a separate township. Although the smallest of the three Pontefract stations it was marginally nearer to the centre of the later town than were the other two, so that shoppers who came to the town would normally alight there; it was also handy for the Park and the Racecourse. The photograph which is taken from an old tinted post-card shows the simple layout looking east from the down platform. There was also a substantial bay platform on the up side.   P COOKSON COLLECTION

One of the few early views of Tanshelf that has come to light shows an immaculate L&YR 0-6-0 No 214 on a very short train which appears to be conveying stone. The occasion of the photograph has not been recorded but there are no less than ten people posing in the picture.   MAUD PHOTOGRAPHY, PONTEFRACT

Race days provided the scenes of greatest activity and this 1950s scene from almost the same location as that in the previous photograph shows three trains. The Class '5' 4-6-0 No 45076 had arrived tender first on the down line with an excursion from the Wakefield direction, but because there was no cross over at the east end of the station had to run down to Pontefract West Junction at Monkhill in order to run round its train; it had then coupled on to the back of the train and is shown drawing its empty coaches into the sidings on the up side. A previous arrival behind a '4F' 0-6-0 had done this manoeuvre and deposited the coaches in the bay platform. The Caprotti 'Black 5' on the left is actually a light engine working down to Goole to bring up an evening freight for Aintree. P COOKSON

Exterior view of Monkhill, the first station in Pontefract opened in 1848. The station building differed considerably from all the others on the WP&G line having been built in a style to harmonize with the ecclesiastical associations of the nearby site of the Cluniac Priory of St John. The down side accommodation was very basic indeed and consisted only of a wooden structure comprising two small waiting rooms. P COOKSON

Not many early photographs appear to have been taken on the L&Y line east of Wakefield, but one that came to light shows the scene at Monkhill looking east from the up platform and taken on 25 April 1902. An up goods train headed by an 0-6-0 locomotive is approaching the station while a sister locomotive stands in the siding next to the goods warehouse, presumably on shunting duties. Of particular note is the burnished hand rails not normally associated with the humble goods locomotive. Just discernible in the down sidings is a birdcage brake.

L&Y SOCIETY COLLECTION

The same view more than 50 years later on a Saturday in 1956. The usual three coach formation of the Goole–Wakefield train has been strengthened to accommodate the Featherstone Rovers Supporters who will use the train for the short ride to Featherstone for a home match. The '8F' in the down sidings has brought coal in from Glass-Houghton colliery for marshalling but the goods yard pilot (just visible in the far background on the warehouse road) is having an easy time of things in the up yard as there was little to do after midday on a Saturday.

P COOKSON

Local Trip working remained in the hands of the Aspinall 0-6-0s even into the late 1950s and this photograph shows one of the Goole engines No 52319 leaving Monkhill on a pick-up freight bound for Wakefield one evening in 1957.

P COOKSON

It was with some considerable surprise that when the L&Y 0-6-0s left the scene in the late 1950s they should have been replaced by an equally venerable species. It was most unexpected when four MS&L locomotives (LNER Class 'J10') were transferred to Goole shed to take over the duties of the L&Y locomotives. No 65142 is shown in the accompanying photograph on the same working as that in the previous picture.

P COOKSON

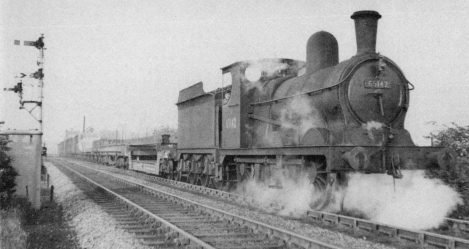

At a point a little west of the junction with the branch to Burton Salmon the LY line crosses over the S&K Joint near Ferrybridge. A Fowler Class 4P 2-6-4T was photographed at this location heading towards Pontefract with an afternoon Goole–Leeds train. Fowler locomotives replaced Stanier 2-6-4T at Goole shed about 1956 and worked the local services until dieselisation in March 1958.

P COOKSON

The west end of Knottingley station. The train running in is a Wakefield–Goole working hauled (rather unusually) by a BR Class 3MT 2-6-0 No 77001 which, at the time, was on temporary loan from Hull to Goole, presumably to cover for a Fowler Class 4P 2-6-4T which would normally be on this train. Knottingley 'A' signal box can be seen on the left and this tall structure was so built to give the signalman a good view of the junction with the Ferrybridge branch on the other side of the main road. P COOKSON

An interior view of Knottingley station taken in 1959. In spite of its imposing size for a small town station, it was by this time very run down. In the quiet of a midsummer's afternoon a WD 2-8-0 is shown rumbling through on an empty wagon train bound for Askern. The station had five platforms, all of which can be seen in the photograph. In its more important days Knottingley was a changing point for passengers using Wakefield–Goole trains and Leeds–Doncaster trains so that at peak times it would have been very busy. P COOKSON

Two views of Knottingley (L&Y and GN Joint) station taken from roughly the same spot on Headlands Lane bridge, but separated in time by approximately half a century. The later view taken in 1956 shows the remains of the engine shed in the left background together with a little of the filled-in turntable pit. The earlier view unfortunately does not show the shed which would have been operational at that time. According to Eric Mason the shed was one of the first L&Y depots to close (1 July 1922).   P COOKSON COLLECTION/P COOKSON

The York & North Midland line represented the culmination of efforts to secure a railway route to the south from the City of York. As early as 1833 this general objective was considered and two years later under the chairmanship of George Hudson, a company was formed with the intention of linking York with the North Midland Railway at Altofts Junction; both the Y & NMR and the NMR obtaining the Royal Assent within a month or so of each other in 1836. George Stephenson was appointed Consulting Engineer for both and he surveyed a route which avoided Tadcaster (which was the only town of any size in that vicinity) and took the Y & NM main line down the Plain of York, into the valley of the river Aire and through Castleford to join the NMR at Altofts Junction. There are no engineering features of note on the line and the present-day traveller on the section from York to Burton Salmon will see hardly any semblance of a cutting or embankment, but on the approach to Castleford there is a substantial embankment crossing the marshy ground around the Nature Reserve of Fairburn Ings, and the river Aire is crossed at this point.

Three important branches were built to give connection with the main line: a North to East branch and a South to East branch in the vicinity of Milford gave access to Selby and Hull from the North and from the South; and at Whitwood, on the outskirts of Castleford, a branch made a northerly connection with the NMR at Methley. A number of other lines were added to the Y & NM system before it became part of the North Eastern Railway in 1854 but all except one (the Burton Salmon to Knottingley link) do not concern us here. The Y & NM was opened in stages but through running to Normanton became possible on 1 July 1840, the date on which the NMR opened to Leeds (Hunslet Lane); the Methley branch was opened later the same month. Although the Hull and Selby line also opened on 1 July 1840, through working from Normanton to Hull was not at first possible because of the unwillingness of the Leeds & Selby company to allow the use of the section of line from Milford Old Junction (Gascoigne Wood Jct) to Selby. Through travel from York to London (Euston) had now become a reality albeit by a circuitous route via Derby, Leicester and Rugby.

The only Y & NM station within the Wakefield area is Castleford, though the present station (which is due for partial demolition at the time of writing) was built by the NER and opened in 1871. The original station was built about ½ mile to the east near to the point where the branch to Ledston diverges from the main line. For a few years the town enjoyed services from York to Leeds, York to Normanton and beyond, and because of the closure by Hudson of the passenger service between Leeds (Marsh Lane) and Selby) the re-routed traffic between Hull and Leeds, using the Methley branch. This last service did not remain for long as the Leeds and Selby line was re-opened to local passenger traffic in 1850. Changes in the NE lines of the Leeds area culminating in the opening of Leeds (New) station in 1869 and the building of the Church Fenton cut-off in the same year, took away some of the remaining traffic. However, by making use of the Methley Joint (GN, NE, L & Y) which had been opened from Lofthouse to Methley Joint Junction (on the Y & NM Whitwood–Methley branch), some four years earlier, Castleford was to gain a new service. This new line enabled the part of the Y & NM branch between the Methley Joint Junction and Methley Junction to be closed to passenger traffic and the institution of a new service of trains to link Castleford with Leeds (Central) via the Methley Joint Line and

the GN system. In addition, by means of the south to east curve at Lofthouse, a service between Wakefield (Westgate) and Castleford was also provided; thus the passenger train of the GNR became a more common sight at Castleford than its counterpart on the NER. The next development at Castleford was the building of the line from Garforth (on the Leeds and Selby), to the Y & NM near to Castleford Old Station. This was projected as the Leeds, Castleford & Pontefract Junction Railway and received its Act in 1873. Its purpose was to open up the colliery district around Kippax and Allerton Bywater. It was eventually opened in 1878 and, though the reason for its building was the transportation of coal, the NER took the opportunity of instituting a passenger service between Leeds (New) and Castleford thereby introducing a few more NE passenger trains to the station. The connection with Pontefract was effected two years later by the construction of a branch from Castleford (New) station to the L & Y Pontefract–Methley branch near to Cutsyke station. Further mention will be made of this later, together with the extension of the Leeds (New)–Castleford service to Pontefract. In 1884 the L & Y began to appear at Castleford (NE) in the working of trains through from Liverpool/Manchester to York/Newcastle via Normanton, but using MR metals between Goose Hill Jct. and Altofts Jct. (the L & Y had, of course, been in evidence at the other station situated in Cutsyke for some years). These trains came to be regarded as the main line trains through Castleford until they eventually ceased (in truncated form) in January 1970.

At this point it is relevant to refer to a railway scheme which never materialised and known variously as the Castleford & Pontefract Railway Company, or the Pontefract & Castleford Railway Company. This was provisionally registered in 1860 with the intention of linking Castleford directly with London via the L & Y at Pontefract and thence to the GN main line at Doncaster. As envisaged the route would only have been about ¾ mile in length and would have run from a point "on the Normanton Road and opposite to the Gatehouse at Glass Houghton, on the L & Y line". The Company claimed that its project would give more expeditious connections to London and the principal towns of Lancaster and York for the manufacturers of the growing industrial town of Castleford. The Great Northern Railway was to have worked the line for the first ten years, providing four trains each way per day, except on Sundays. However it was never built and connection between Castleford (NE) and Pontefract was eventually made by the Leeds, Castleford & Pontefract Junction Railway which opened in 1878.

The 1960s and 1970s saw a number of changes to passenger traffic patterns at Castleford with the Methley Joint line closing to regular passenger traffic in November 1964. The station was without a Leeds service until October 1968 when the service was transferred over the newly re-opened Y & NM branch from Whitwood Junction to Methley Junction, and the trains routed to Leeds City. A change which was to affect the main line through Castleford occurred in 1973 with the beginning of the summer timetable. As a result of an agreement between the National Coal Board and British Rail with regard to subsidence of lines caused by mining, the main North-East–South-West passenger traffic which had hitherto used the S & K Jt line between York and Sheffield was transferred to the Y & NM route via Castleford and Normanton; the intention being to upgrade the latter for high speed running, and allowing the S

& K to be affected by subsidence due to extensive mining in the Dearne Valley. This state of affairs did not last for long however, and by the end of the decade traffic had filtered back to the S & K line so that at the time of writing, the situation is again as it was before 1973. This however will change yet again by the summer of 1984 when the traffic will be diverted to the new main line by-passing Selby. The only passenger service now regularly serving Castleford is the one from Leeds to Pontefract and Knottingley (with about half the trains running through to Goole)

and involving a reversal at Castleford, but the Y & NM line still sees a few summer trains running through to Scarborough from Wakefield and calling at the station. The days of competing services have now gone in today's unified railway system, and it is hard to appreciate that not so long ago the railway traveller from Castleford had a choice of three different services to Leeds: the GN via the Methley Joint, the NE via Garforth, and the L & Y (from Cutsyke) via Methley Junction.

Castleford (Central) station looking towards Normanton in 1958. This station was opened in 1871 the original one having been sited some distance to the east nearer to the junction with the Kippax branch. The station name had 'Central' added to it in 1952 in order to distinguish it from Castleford (Cutsyke) on the Pontefract–Methley branch of the L&Y. Beyond the signal box the branch to Cutsyke Junction diverges to the left.
P COOKSON

This photograph shows a Leeds Central–Castleford Central Saturday only train arriving at Castleford in September 1958. The service had been dieselized by this time and the only remaining steam-hauled trains were the mid-day (Saturdays only) and a Saturday excepted early evening train for workers returning from Leeds. The 'N1' 0-6-2T were thin on the ground at this time but had given long service on these trains and No 69450 in particular was usually to be found in very clean external condition up to withdrawal. Other locomotive classes commonly seen on these trains included ex GC Class 'C14' and ex GN 'C12'.
P COOKSON

The NE atmosphere was preserved at Castleford by the presence of Class 'Q6' 0-8-0 Nos 63451 and 63395 on coal train duties. Much of the coal produced in the Castleford and Pontefract area was worked to Gascoigne Wood marshalling yard by this type of locomotive (allocated to Selby shed), ably assisted in earlier years by Class 'Q5' and 'J27' types.
P COOKSON

Many excursions from the Castleford area started from Kippax and also served Bowers and Ledston before gaining the main line at either Garforth or Castleford. In the case of the east coast destinations e.g. Bridlington and Scarborough, the workings entailed reversal, and locomotives worked tender first off the branch. In the photograph an unusual pairing of a 'B1' and a 'Jubilee' head for Castleford from Kippax with an excursion bound for the East Coast. The locomotives are Nos 61086 and 45581 *Bihar and Orissa*.
M BALDWIN

One of the ex GCR Class 'B4' 4-6-0s No 1483, which settled in the West Riding in LNER days, is shown in this 1949 photograph of a coal train coming off the L&Y branch from Lofthouse Junction and passing Methley South Station.
B PARF

The branch from the L&Y line was quite steeply graded and coal trains were sometimes banked up to the Methley Joint line. The 'B4' in the previous photograph was being banked by the unidentified 'J6' 0-6-0 shown here passing through Methley South station.
B PARF

The NE freight from Wrenthorpe yard to Gascoigne Wood is shown crossing over the North Midland main line at Methley behind ex NE Class 'Q6' 0-8-0 No 63429. Midland signals on a lattice post are in evidence just beyond the overbridge.   B PARR

Most of the station buildings at Methley South are visible in this photograph of Class 'B1' 4-6-0 No 61388 heading a coal train on the Castleford line and bound for Gascoigne Wood. The strongly Great Northern appearance is exemplified by the signal box.   P COOKSON

The use of rail transport by the local industries in the Wakefield area can be traced back to the mid-eighteenth century when an advertisement of 1745 indicated that there was a waggonway in the Stanley area which was used to carry coal from a colliery to the River Calder at Bottomboat. Other waggonways were built for the same purpose and in 1798 the most famous of them all, the Lake Lock Rail Road was opened. The Lake Lock can probably be regarded as the first public railway in the country. It was built to a track gauge of 3ft 4in using, in 1828, 40 lb per yard rails. The waggons used at this time were called half waggons as they only carried 1⅛ tons of coal compared to the 2½ tons in the normal size of waggon.

Two other major waggonways, or tramroads, at this time were those built by the colliery owners Robert Smithson and William Fenton to transport their pits' products from the Ardsley and Kirkhamgate area to the River Calder at Thornes Wharf in Wakefield. There was considerable friction between the two mine owners and this led them to build separate tramroads along the side of Alverthorpe Beck down to the Calder. The track gauge of Smithson's Tramroad was about 4ft 0in and the rail laid on stone blocks, some of which can still be seen today, lying in the beck. The loaded waggons were probably allowed to run down to the river using gravity with the empties being hauled back by oxen. At the wharf, a small yard was eventually built and in 1849 the L & Y constructed a wagon lift adjacent to their main line just west of Kirkgate station so that interchange of goods could be made with the tramroad and river traffic.

Since the days of the industrial revolution, Wakefield has had a great variety of industries and many of these were served by the main line railways and several had their own railway systems. Of particular note was the system which served the firms which were located along Calder Vale Road adjacent to the south side of Kirkgate station. Sidings were laid between the station and the road and from these spurs branched off into the various works yards. The firm of E, Green & Son had quite an extensive system which had the use of the Company's own locomotives. In the early years of this century, the firm generated so much traffic with the sale of its products that the GNR designed and built a batch of special wagons solely for its use. Another works in the area was that of the Calder Vale Steel Boat Company. One of its products was a ship's lifeboat and quantities of these were loaded onto wagons for delivery, via the main line railways, to the major shipyards. On the bank of the Calder in the Thornes area was the works of Hodgson &

Hudswell Clarke saddle tank *Standback No 3* leaves the BR/NCB exchange sidings near Horbury & Ossett station with a rake of wagons for Hartley Bank colliery on 29 April 1966. The L&Y main line runs in the background across the picture.   M BRADLEY

Simpson, soap manufacturers. The factory had its own self-contained railway system utilizing steam locomotives for haulage. The site is now the premises of the Johnson & Nephew Company. Whenever the connection between railways and industry in the Wakefield area are mentioned, it is inevitable that sooner or later the name of Charles Roberts will turn up. Roberts founded the railway wagon building company which bore his name, in 1856. The first factory was at Ings Road, Wakefield and it was not long before the company became a major supplier to the railway industry. In 1873, the company moved to new premises situated between the L & Y main line and the Barnsley branch at Horbury Junction. Up to 1885 most railway wagons had been fitted with solid "dumb" buffers but, in that year, new regulations came into use which stipulated that spring buffers should be fitted. The Charles Roberts Company built the very first wagon fitted with spring buffers bought by the L & Y. This vehicle carried L & Y registration number 1. By 1927 the works was building vast quantities of wagons with one standard 12 ton coal wagon being produced every 25 minutes. Also at that time, every component required to build a wagon was manufactured in the Horbury Junction works. The Company was very involved with the hiring out of wagons and up to 1948 had a fleet of over 30,000 vehicles available for this purpose. During both world wars the factory was used to manufacture items for the war effort and in the second of those conflicts the items included Naval shells, mortar bombs and armour-piercing shot plus 1300 Churchill tanks and parts for ships being built on the Humber. Charles Roberts was always in the forefront of wagon design and in 1944 was contracted to build the prototype of the major railway companies' new standard 4-wheel tank wagon. This was tested by each of the "big four" and eventually accepted by them. The Company was involved with the manufacture of hopper wagons from the early days of this century and in 1937 they built what was thought to be the largest hopper on British railways at that time. This was for Imperial Chemical Industries and was designed to carry 43 tons of limestone. Passenger carrying vehicles have also been built and these included trams for Blackpool and Khartoum and, in the mid-1950s, standard coaches for British Railways. In 1974 the railway wagon interests and half of the Horbury Junction works were bought by Procor (UK) Ltd, a company which up to that time, had been in the business of wagon fleet hire but not manufacture. Considerable numbers of wagons of all shapes and sizes have been built since that time including massive 100 ton bogie tankers and double-deck car transporters. The latter vehicles, named 'Procars' were at the time of writing, the longest rigid freight vehicles running on British Railways, being 24.206m (79ft 5in) over buffers.

The longest lasting industrial railways in the area are those at the collieries. Although many have disappeared particularly in recent years, there are survivors and in fact the last steam engines in operation remained until the early 1980s. Steam made a short comeback for twelve months between November 1981 and November 1982 when the Hunslet Engine Company tested an automatic underfeed stoker on an NCB Locomotive at Wheldale Colliery. Today the NCB uses diesel shunters for working its yards but evidence of earlier forms of power can still be seen. One example is the rope-hauled tramway which ran between the Monckton pits at Havercroft and Royston. Only a short distance from Felkirk church can be seen the girder bridge where the tramway crossed the cutting of the Dearne Valley line. Beyond this bridge can be seen some of the pulleys which guided the continuous wire rope at the point where the track curved round a bend. The biggest industrial railway in the area was the East & West Yorkshire Union Railway, which, apart from a few remaining earthworks, has been virtually wiped off the map.

East Ardsley No 2 poses at East Ardsley Colliery just before the First World War. This inside cylinder 0-6-0ST was built by Manning Wardle in 1893 and carried builders' number 1267. It spent all of its working life at the colliery being rebuilt in 1911 and 1942 and finally being withdrawn from service in June 1958. The loco was cut up in 1960.
GRIFFITH
COLLECTION

Appendices

OPENING AND CLOSING DATES OF WAKEFIELD AREA STATIONS

Station	Company	Opening Date	Closure Date	Notes
Ardsley	BW & L	5.10.1857	2.11.1964	
Lofthouse & Outwood	MJR	1858	13.6.1960	
Stanley	MJR	1.5.1869	2.11.1964	
Methley Joint (South)	MJR	1.5.1869	7.3.1960	
Ossett	BW & L	7.4.1864	7.9.1964	
Flushdyke	BW & L	7.4.1862	5.5.1941	
Alverthorpe	BW & L	10.1872	5.4.1954	
Wakefield Westgate	GNR MS & L MR	5.10.1857		
Sandal (GN)	WR & G	1.2.1866	4.11.1957	
Hare Park & Crofton	WR & G	11.1885	4.2.1952	
(Wintersett &) Ryhill	MS & L	1.9.1882	22.9.1930	Ryhill to 1/3/1927
Nostell	WR & G	1.2.1866	29.10.1951	
Fitzwilliam	LNER	1.6.1937	6.11.1967	Reopened 1/3/1982
Hemsworth	WR & G	1.2.1866	6.11.1967	
South Elmsall	WR & G	1.2.1866		
Altofts & Whitwood	MR	1.9.1870		
Normanton	NMR	1.7.1840		
Oakenshaw	NMR	1.7.1840	1.6.1870	Wakefield to 1/3/1841
Sandal & Walton	MR	1.6.1870	12.6.1961	Walton from 30/9/1951
Middlestown	MR	10.11.1905	4.5.1968	Goods only station
Crigglestone	MR	3.7.1905	8.1968	Goods only station
Horbury & Ossett	M & L	5.10.1840	5.1.1970	
Millfield Road	LMS	11.7.1927	6.11.1961	
Crigglestone (West)	LYR	1.1.1850	13.9.1965	
Horbury Junction	LYR	1.1.1850	11.7.1927	
Wakefield (Kirkgate)	M & L	5.10.1840		Kirkgate from 23/8/1853
Crofton (L & Y)	LYR	1.11.1853	30.11.1931	
Ryhill Halt	LYR	3.6.1912	10.9.1951	
Sharlston	LYR	1869	3.3.1958	
Featherstone	WP & G	1.4.1848	2.1.1967	
Pontefract) Tanshelf	LYR	9.1871	2.1.1967	Pontefract added 1/12/1936
Pontefract (Monkhill)	WP & G	1.4.1848		Monkhill added 1/12/1936
Methley Junction (L & Y)	WP & G	1.10.1849	4.10.1943	
Castleford (L & Y)	LYR	1860	7.10.1968	Cutsyke added 15/9/52
Knottingley	WP & G	1.4.1848		
Castleford (NE)	Y & NM	1.7.1840		Central added 15/9/52
Ledston (E)	LC & PJ	12.8.1878	22.1.1951	
Ferrybridge	NER	1.5.1882	13.9.1965	
Pontefract (Baghill)	S & K	1.7.1879		Baghill added 1/12/1936
Ackworth	S & K	1.7.1879	2.7.1951	
Moorthorpe & Sth Kirkby	S & K	1.7.1879		
Upton & North Elmsall	H & B	27.7.1885	1.1.1932	
Hemsworth (H & B)	H & B	1.7.1891	1.1.1932	
Moorhouse & Sth Elmsall	H & B	23.8.1902	6.4.1929	

Notes:		
	BW & L	Bradford Wakefield and Leeds, – later GNR
	MJR	Methley Joint Railway – GNR, NER, LYR
	WR & G	West Riding and Grimsby – GNR / MS & LR
	WP & G	Wakefield Pontefract and Goole – later LYR
	LC & PJ	Leeds, Castleford & Pontefract Junction – later NER
	S & K	Swinton and Knottingley Joint – later MR/NER

The opening dates given refer to the first day of public service; official openings and the beginning of goods services were often earlie
Closure dates given refer to the official closure; the last day of service was commonly two days earlier if there was no Sunday servic